Dr. Sandra Kennedy is a wonderful woman of God whom my wife and I have known and respected for many years. I thoroughly enjoyed reading her book on the blood of Jesus, and I highly recommend it to anyone who is interested in living in victory every day—and not just on Sunday! When you start drawing on the power of the blood regularly, you are going to see change in yourself, your circumstances, and even in the lives of your loved ones. This is an excellent book, and I hope you enjoy it as much as I did.

—Dr. Jesse Duplantis
Jesse Duplantis Ministries
Hammond, Louisiana

Are you willing to think "out of the box"—even about the blood of Jesus? Sandra Kennedy is! She offers an exciting and challenging understanding of the efficacy of the blood of Jesus. All believers rest in the efficacy of the blood of Jesus for salvation yet fail to apply it to unconquered areas in their personal lives. Kennedy stresses that as believer priests we may also use this authority to apply the blood over the lives of our family and wayward loved ones. This is worth the read!

—Dr. Iverna M. Tompkins
Iverna Tompkins Ministries
Scottsdale, Arizona

D1510927

I am delighted to write this for my admired friend and colleague, Dr. Sandra Kennedy. As I read this book I could hear this anointed servant-teacher pouring out her own heart to her beloved flock. She is a passionate and transparent seeker after God. Her heart is pure and fixed on Jesus, and it shows in this book. *Hope for the Heart* is a plea for God's people to not only experience the cleansing work of the Spirit but also to exercise their priesthood in helping others to a life of forgiveness and power. I heartily recommend this book to preachers, teachers, leaders, and all who seek a deeper experience of Christ and His love.

—Dr. Ronald E. Cottle
Founder and President Emeritus
Beacon University, Columbus, Georgia

HOPE

for the

HEART

ele ele ele ele

Sandra G. Kennedy

CREATION
HOUSE
A STRANG COMPANY

HOPE FOR THE HEART by Sandra G. Kennedy
Published by Creation House
A Strang Company
600 Rinehart Road
Lake Mary, Florida 32746
www.creationhouse.com

All Scripture quotations are from the King James Version of the Bible.

Word definitions are derived from *Strong's Exhaustive Concordance of the Bible*, ed. James Strong, Nashville, TN: Thomas Nelson Publishers, 1997.

Cover design by Terry Clifton

Library of Congress Control Number: 2006936893
International Standard Book Number: 978-1-59979-159-3

First Edition

07 08 09 10 11 — 987654321
Printed in the United States of America

This book is dedicated to all the wonderful people, especially those in my church, who have taken the teachings on the cleansing power of the blood to heart, applied them to their lives, and have seen tremendous victory. And to all who encouraged me to put the teachings in writing so that others may discover the cleansing power of the blood of Jesus, know how to release that power in their lives, and walk in victory.

Acknowledgments

I would like to offer a special word of appreciation to Rev. John Stocker whose teachings from over twenty years ago have given me great inspiration.

My sincerest thanks to Charlene Kiraly, Velda Schirhart, and Lynette Whitlock whose dedication and efforts have helped make this book a reality.

Contents

Foreword

Dr. Sandra Kennedy is a wonderful woman of God whom my wife and I have known and respected for many years. She has that unique ability to put you at ease, make you feel welcome, and share the Word in a real and easy-to-understand way. On top of that, the woman just flat makes me smile! This book comes from her heart and her perspective as a psychologist, therapist, counselor, and anointed minister of the gospel, and it will show you a different side of the blood of Jesus—one that reaches beyond the sinner's prayer and into the everyday, ongoing life of the believer.

Sandra's book addresses some of the issues we all deal with from time to time. It is filled with the Word, her wisdom, and her wonderful personality. I highly recommend it to anyone who is interested in living in victory every day—and not just on Sunday! I believe that, when you start drawing on the power of the blood regularly, you are going to see change in yourself, your circumstances, and even in the lives of your loved ones.

Whether you have been saved five minutes or fifty years, you are going to learn something from this book. I did, and I enjoyed every minute of it. The blood of Jesus is what gives every one of us hope for today, tomorrow, and the far-off future. The blood *never* loses its power—it remains a continual source of grace, mercy, and power that we can draw upon and see results. The blood cleans up our mind. It cleans up our body. It cleans up situations that we don't know what to do about! The blood *is* power, and in this book you will learn how to use it in a way you may never have thought of before. Sandra has some great revelation about the ongoing cleansing power of the blood that is going to lift your heart and make your journey in this life easier and a lot more joyful.

So, sit down, get comfortable, and get ready to start seeing yourself through the powerful, precious, and finished work of the blood. You are going to learn how to stop trying to become what you already are—free—and start living the good life that Jesus came to give to you. As she would say, it is time to start flying with the eagles and stop crash-landing with the turkeys! Are you ready to learn something new? Good! This is a book and an author that I highly recommend to you. To me, it just doesn't get much better than Dr. Sandra Kennedy. I hope you enjoy her book as much as I did. May God bless you in every way.

—Dr. Jesse Duplantis

Introduction

WHAT YOU ARE ABOUT TO read will put many of you on the edge of your seats with excitement. Over the years, this message of hope has brought great freedom and peace to those who have embraced it. So many of us desire a closer walk with our Father, yet something has held us back. We have repented before the Lord Jesus, and He has forgiven us faithfully. His blood has washed us clean from sin, but something still darkens the chasms of our heart, and we remain trapped. However, knowledge of the great Bible truth I am about to share will successfully lift the stains of sin from your heart. When this truth is applied to your personal life, it will enable you to climb to higher levels in your relationship with almighty God.

As I travel in ministry, I see people who are hungry for more of God. Everywhere I go, there is a small group of people who are ready to quit "playing church" and get serious with the Lord. This group pulls on the anointing. They are ready to do whatever is necessary to lay down the sin that has entangled them and walk deeper into His marvelous light. These precious saints are forgetting themselves and falling in love with Jesus all over again. They want to worship and adore our heavenly Savior in a new and vibrant way truly pleasing to Him. They are striving to know the One who released them from the darkness that held them captive, and will empower them to live a lifestyle expressing the kingdom of God.

This is the remnant, emerging as a bride, cleansed and beautiful, prepared for her Bridegroom. This is so glorious to behold. Such excitement fills my heart when I witness the moving of God's Spirit in the hearts of these brothers and sisters who are receiving this truth about the blood of Jesus. For those of you who hunger and thirst for a closer relationship with the Father—for those of you who desire to walk the higher road with your heart *completely* clean and free from your past—this message is for you.

There truly is hope for your heart.

one

What's Wrong Here?

I HAVE BEEN TEACHING GOD'S WORD since I was nineteen years old. During these many years, I have been in a position to watch the lives of people, who deal with the Word of God, change, much as I have watched my own. Initially, we are often so excited about the Word and its impact, but we have a tendency to gradually regress into our former habits by letting slip the Word's place of importance in our lives. For whatever reason, we do not stay plugged in to the truths of God. Perhaps we believe that these truths and experiences will carry us the rest of our lives, but they will not unless they are continually embraced and refreshed.

Many years ago, before I accepted God's call into full-time ministry, I spent fourteen years of my life working for my home state of Georgia as a psychologist, therapist, and counselor. During that time, I held the position of district director of mental health and mental retardation centers around the state. While in this capacity, I saw multitudes of people experiencing every imaginable kind of problem.

I witnessed the devastation those problems caused in their lives, and how hard it was for them to rebound to normalcy after facing their difficulties. But the thing that absolutely amazed me, and still does even today, is that as a pastor, I saw the same patterns in the lives of saints that I saw in the world. I still see the same struggles and problems in the church that I saw outside the church years ago.

As a whole, I do not even see Christians rebounding or *desiring* to rebound any faster than those who do not have the Spirit of grace to assist them. To be frank, I often do not see any difference at all, and to me that is a very sad and scary thing. How can this possibly be? We are Christians, in the body of Christ. We have the Holy Spirit actually living within us. We have been raised up to sit with Him in heavenly places. For us to be in the mess we are in, there must be something terribly wrong.

We must be missing something that God has already provided for us, because Jesus' work on the cross is already complete. There is nothing more that He must accomplish to defeat the devil. My brothers and sisters, we are supposed to be victorious as members of God's elite family.

There are thousands upon thousands of people who claim Jesus as Lord and Savior but are not walking in the power of their salvation. We definitely are not enjoying the benefits of our salvation, which Jesus shed His blood to purchase for us. Herein lies the problem: the Word of God and the Blood of Jesus will bring us to a place of total victory. If the Bible is just a book—an everyday book we are not really supposed to understand, and are only supposed to read in church on Sunday morning—then let's face it, we are wasting our time. The Bible is God's Word, and it will accomplish what God sent it to do (Isa. 55:11). We do not need to make things so complicated or chase such abstract theories that only a handful of us are ever able to comprehend the simpleness of God's Word. We just need to say, "This is what it says; this is what it means; and this is how it works," and then, with the help of almighty God, do it.

Let me tell you something: I enjoy my salvation. I enjoy being saved. I have been to hell and back a few times, and I can tell you, the "back" trip is much better. Thank God for the cleansing power of the blood of the Lamb. He has set me free; glory to God! I was a mess before Jesus got a hold of me, and I have even been a mess a few times since. But, praise God, the power of the blood of Jesus has changed my life from deep within.

It did not happen overnight. Sometimes it took a little while for that blood to penetrate, to break through the crust of unbelief and cleanse me of the garbage I had within me. It did eventually bring victory, thank God. It kept working as long as I put it to work. But in truth, when I stopped, it stopped.

We should be walking on a higher plane than the world. After all, we are supposed to be seated with Jesus in heavenly places. (See Eph. 2:6.) If we are not there, then we are the ones who have moved, because according to God's Word, that is where He has seated us.

One of my greatest joys is to look out at the congregation and see people who, like myself, have walked the hard path in life. Despite all odds, they have made it to a place of victory. I see those who have been in utter darkness, those to whom life has dealt harsh blows. I see those who were in the middle of the sea when the storm hit, and though the storm tried to take them under, they made it to the other side. I love to see God working in the lives of these people. They simply hear what they need to hear and do what they need to do, and God does the rest. God is always faithful.

Just by living in this crazy world it is easy to find ourselves in a mess—in a pit, with no apparent way out. We normally do not have to go looking very far for trouble. It is highly adept at putting us in its crosshairs. But, hope can begin to flicker deep within us when we embrace the Word of God; hope not only of escaping the trouble, but hope that God really does not leave us nor forsake us. What a fabulous truth that is! Being a Christian should be synonymous with victory, no matter the source of the trouble.

I have found myself in places where I thought He left me. Have you ever been to that lonesome place where you thought even God had given up on you? Of course, He does not leave us, but it sure feels that way sometimes, doesn't it? We just get so caught up in the situations and circumstances we are facing, that we wind up blocking His actions. Believe me, we have all done it a million times. But, one word from God, one word that pierces our hearts, can change our lives in an instant. There should never be hopelessness in God's people, but sadly, I see it all too often. God knows no impossibilities; the problem is that *we see them.*

Today, according to the headlines of our newspapers, being called a Christian means little; the name is thrown about all too casually. But in my view, if we are going to be called "Christian" after our Lord Jesus, we need to live like Him. It makes no sense for us to go around talking about victory, but not having any real victory in our lives. We have to walk this thing out and be the lights in the dark places of this world. Glory to God, we can do it!

The early Christians certainly lived out their lives with

great faith and godliness. Their presence had a tremendous impact on the civilization of their day. The Christlikeness of the new birth was evident and real to them. Their relationship with Jesus was so real to them that everything about them changed. They were overcomers who lived out their faith in such perfection that everybody was either for them or against them—there was no middle ground.

It was very difficult being a Christian back then. We act like it is worse now, but in truth, thousands were killed then just for being faithful to God. They lived persecuted lives, yet the Bible says they turned the world upside down for Christ. (See Acts 17:6.) Why is it that in today's world, Christians have not been able to make a similar impact and cause the eyes of the world to gaze on this life-changing Jesus within us? Be assured, every victory is always wrapped in the blood of the Lamb. In this book, we will press deeper into His immeasurable truth. Praise God!

The blood of Jesus is precious and holy in the sight of almighty God. After all, it was the sacrifice and death of His beloved Son on the cross at Calvary that saved us all—every man, woman, and child—from destruction. We learn that we must come quickly to the altar, ask forgiveness for our sins, claim our forgiveness with our mouths, and walk in the forgiveness of our sins. As believers, His blood is the key to our wonderful salvation, and we must embrace and esteem the blood with honor. It has the power to reconcile the chasm between unholy people and our holy God. The blood of Jesus draws us nigh unto Him and invites us into the household of God as sons and daughters. What a privilege! Glory to His name forever!

The blood enables God to forgive us of our sins, and to cleanse us from all unrighteousness. That is certainly a true and exciting reality for us. But there is another aspect of the cleansing power of the blood that I have not heard discussed much.

When the Lord first uncovered this revelation to me, I began remembering crises in my own life through which I had successfully passed. I discovered with joy that the Lord had been leading me down this pathway a great many years, although I was not consciously aware of it. Isn't it interesting how we can know things in our spirit before we know them in our heads? God's mercy is beyond our comprehension. He is absolutely wonderful.

As I began to teach my church these principles, and they began to grasp and apply them to their own lives, this revelation brought about more change in the hearts of the people than anything I have ever taught. I had never seen so many positive changes take place so fast; it was absolutely astounding. There were so many turnarounds in family situations—turnarounds that actually lasted. Do you know what I mean? We can have turnarounds today, but then tomorrow go back the other way. The changes I have witnessed in the lives of people have kept them going the right way since this teaching on the blood of Jesus has come forth.

It has been amazing. As a matter of fact, we took a two-week period and did a quick test. We learned how to use the blood of Jesus as a priest, and apply that precious blood of the Lamb to situations that were "messed up," and to people who did not know the Lord. Out of the approximately one hundred people who participated in this test, approximately 70 percent of them saw positive results in that short period of time. Some of the situations and people had been prayed over for many years, but in a two-week time period the people saw God change them. Glory!

So, do I have your interest, now? Great! Then let's get started, shall we?

two

Listen Up

Hᴏw ᴍᴀɴʏ ᴏғ ᴜs ʜᴀᴠᴇ had a failure? How many of us have had more than one? It is unanimous, I assure you. Most of us have had more failures than we would like to admit, and all of us have regrets. The Lord showed me one thing in particular, in my own life and in the lives of others, that when we fail or sin and come to Him repentant, we always receive forgiveness through the shed blood of Jesus Christ. Sometimes when we attempt to reestablish our relationship with Him it seems so difficult to get past those failures. It does not seem to matter how much we pray, how much others pray for us, or how well we understand that God forgives us of our sins by the blood of the Lamb and cleanses us from all unrighteousness. Most of the time, we just cannot seem to get past our failures. It is like we are always dragging something behind us, or that there is something *dark* hovering over us. Yes, we have certainly asked Jesus to forgive us, and He has been faithful to do just that. But, it seems that "thing" is still there for everybody to see. Can you relate to what I am saying?

It is like having on a piece of clothing that we know is stained. It might be that the stain is inconspicuous, but *we know it is there.* That forgiven sin seems to be the same way for us—it stays with us like a dark cloud and hinders us from walking in the absolute freedom that the blood of Jesus provides. That, my friend, is the nature of sin. Yet, the Word of God states the blood has set us free from sin and the power of that sin.

As I look back through my life, I notice when sins—though forgiven—would get a grip on me and hold me captive. I know that I am not alone. Each of us would have to admit that our past sins continue to haunt us, and we still feel dirty, don't we? We know with our heads that the blood of Jesus is enough, yet, we think we still ought to somehow pay penance for those transgressions. We feel like we need to do something more, repent again, cry a little more, or tell God how rotten we are—something.

You know, I can remember going to camp meetings years ago. I always shied away from meetings with prophets in those days. I never liked going to where the prophets were. I realize there are many people who seek out persons with that prophetic gift, but I have never been one of them. I was convinced (erroneously, of course) that they were going to point their finger at me and expose me before the crowd. But the exposure that terrified me concerned sins for which I had already been forgiven. I truly felt that everyone could still see all those things that I had done; that a "guilty" sign was bolted to my forehead. Today, it is a different story; I just love prophets! It is wonderful to be clean. I tell you, it is absolutely wonderful to be truly cleansed by the blood.

So what is the problem? We know that God does not hold our forgiven sin against us. The Bible emphatically declares that. Because of the sacrifice of Jesus, God *chooses* not to remember our sin. Now, *people* continue to hold things against us, but God does not. The work of the cross has been completed. So what is the problem? Simple. We just have not gone deep enough.

We are now dealing with the *nature of sin*. We have to look deeper into the power of the blood of Jesus, and that is the very thing we are going to discuss in this book. Yes, something *does* attach itself to us. We are going to find out from the Word of God what that something is and how to break its power over us. We are going to find out that we truly are priests before almighty God, and that we can and should be applying the blood over ourselves and those who are not walking in victory. Praise God forevermore! But, now we need to talk about something else.

> Wherefore lay apart all filthiness and superfluity of naughtiness, and receive with meekness the engrafted word, which is able to save your souls. But be ye doers of the word, and not hearers only, deceiving your own selves. For if any be a hearer of the word, and not a doer, he is like unto a man beholding his natural face in a glass: For he beholdeth himself, and goeth his way, and straightway forgetteth what manner of man he was. But whoso looketh into the perfect law of liberty, and continueth therein, he being not a forgetful hearer, but a doer of the work, this man shall be blessed in his deed.
>
> —JAMES 1:21–25

The Bible talks about being doers of the Word, not hearers only. This scripture says that if we want to be blessed, we cannot just hear, we must *do* what we hear. Even if we read

11

and hear the Word every day of the week, if we are not putting those words into practice, we will not reap the benefits of obedience. Many church members are only hearers of God's Word. We sit on the pews, and we hear and hear and hear. By far, the majority of us hear the Word, at least with our natural ears. Churches are saturated with hearers, but hearers do not necessarily "do." People come and hear, and some even say, "Yes, Amen." Some nod their heads in agreement with what they have heard, while others simply nod heads and then drift soundly off to sleep. When they leave the sanctuary, they leave everything they have heard on the pew behind them.

Almost 85 percent of the people in this nation attend church once a week on Sunday morning, although they do not read their Bible, nor pray more than a few minutes per day. Those are national statistics. As a matter of fact, they think hearing some pastor for one hour a week is far more than enough. Most would say that they are Christians in right standing with God, but they live the same way they did out in the world. *Is it really possible for God to move into our spirits, but no changes take place in our behavior?* We cannot walk with God, experience fellowship with God, or understand the things of God, and be just a hearer.

God works with those who are hearers *and* doers of the Word. What does that mean? It means applying the Word of God to our day-to-day living. God needs people who not only hear, but do what they hear. To be honest with you, God holds us accountable for truth once we have heard it and understood it, whether we do it or not. In that situation, our disobedience turns into a curse, meaning God cannot bless us.

We all have a tendency to hear God's Word initially with great excitement, but due to a multitude of reasons we often quickly let go of the truths we just heard. We must not let go but hold on to these great truths. Too often we have an experience with God and gain a degree of freedom, and then we think that is going to carry us the rest of our life. Not so! We all have discovered those same besetting sins will begin to come back on us, and we must once again battle for our freedom. The Scripture is very clear, but let me repeat: if we want to be blessed, we must not only be hearers of the Word, but also doers. Regardless of what is happening in your life right now, if you will actually do what the Word says to do, your life will be permanently transformed.

Let me share with you another one of our problems. Even though we are spirit people, we are so led by what we see, hear, and feel in the natural realm that we keep getting pulled back in that direction. We have to constantly pray and talk to ourselves about being new creatures in Christ Jesus. Let's get really honest, shall we? Surrounded by the power of these natural influences, it is difficult for us to operate with any consistency in the reality of the truth that we really are spirit beings made in the image of almighty God. All of us struggle with this to some degree or another. We get nuggets of God's truth that drop into our hearts, and we endeavor to hold on to them, but we are constantly dropping back into the natural realm. Face it—most of us are more tuned in to the natural arena of life because it is more real to us than the world of the spirit.

Victory is a spiritual thing. We tend to believe that victory is tied up in the natural world because we can see the blessings of victory in the lives of people around us, whether it be money, good health, or whatever. But victory does not take place in the natural realm first. It is first birthed in our spirit. Our flesh is an enemy of our spirit. It constantly fights us. Although we will never have complete success ruling our flesh, there is a dimension in which we can truly be overcomers now in this life. It is all wrapped up in what we see and hear. But we need to scrutinize what we see and hear. Now look with me at Matthew 13:13–15:

> Therefore speak I to them in parables: because they seeing see not; and hearing they hear not, neither do they understand. And in them is fulfilled the prophecy of Esaias, which saith, By hearing ye shall hear, and shall not understand; and seeing ye shall see, and shall not perceive: For this people's heart is waxed gross, and their ears are dull of hearing, and their eyes they have closed; lest at any time they should see with their eyes, and hear with their ears, and should understand with their heart, and should be converted, and I should heal them.
>
> —MATTHEW 13:13–15

Now, we understand that God created us to walk in truth—to walk in His image—but people dulled their ears and closed their eyes. Write this on the tablet of your heart: we were made to walk with God and hear Him speaking to us. Think about how wonderful that is. He desires to share His heart with us and communicate with us as friends. *Oh my—Lord Jesus, You are so good to us. Thank You.*

It remains true that we can turn our ears off and choose not to hear and reject the truth as that scripture so clearly states. When we do that, we leave ourselves vulnerable for our hearts to be hardened and to be tempted to fall away from God. Hear me—when we reject God's truth, we become spiritually blind and deaf. It does not matter how saved we are.

We will start stumbling, walking about in darkness. This is not about going to heaven after we die, it is about Christians rejecting the truth they have heard, and refusing to allow it to change their lives.

There is a multitude of reasons why we do that. Sometimes, the truth does not line up with what we have been taught. It may not agree with denominational doctrines that we are aligned with, or we may know somebody for whom the Word did not "seem to work." No matter the reason, excuses will only keep us from walking in victory in a way that exemplifies the abundant life Jesus died to give us.

When we hear a message and say, "Wow, wasn't that good?" but yet we fail to apply the principles to our daily lives, we need to beware. We are inviting spiritual blindness and deafness. In one sense, every time we refuse to be doers of the Word, we are saying that we do not consider the Word important enough for us to put it into practice in our lives. Perhaps it would be to our advantage to reread the history of Israel and the examples of the old covenant that were written for our instruction.

In the same way that we can reject truth, we can also embrace lies. We must learn to compare what we hear and see, and even what we already believe, against what God's Word actually says. We can be sincere, yet be sincerely wrong, and believe something completely contrary to the Word. While we love and honor our pastors, we need to read and find out what the Word of God says for ourselves. I will let you in on a secret. This may shock you, but *we pastors do not know everything*. Surprised? I know it is hard to believe, but yes, it is true. We are just people, like you, but people to whom God has given the responsibility of shepherding His flock. Be assured, we always need to be learning for ourselves what the Word says. Now, let's look at another important scripture:

> Take heed, brethren, lest there be in any of you an evil heart of unbelief, in departing from the living God.
>
> —HEBREWS 3:12

This passage is not written to the sinner, but to those in the church who have made Jesus Christ the Lord of their lives—that's us. It says that we had better take heed to something. An evil heart of unbelief can cause us to depart from the living God. That is a pretty serious warning, my brothers and sisters. When we begin to think that a situation or a circumstance occurring in our life is bigger than the power of God, we have, at that moment, invited a dangerous seed of unbelief into our life.

All of us take an initial blast of unbelief when some hideous thing hits our life, and we may be thrown off balance for a time. But however long we stay tuned in to that unbelief will depend on what is actually in our heart at the time. If we stay tuned in to the negative side of life, we are just watering seeds of unbelief, which will produce negative thoughts and emotions within us. I am telling you, church—that is a very frightening thing to me, because we live in a world that is saturated with negativism. Naturally speaking, all of us tend to go that way, but negativism works against God in our lives. We really have to exert effort and strive to stay centered in faith.

I assure you, if we really knew what dangers we were dealing with through unbelief, we would refuse to allow it to operate in our lives. Our God is a God of possibilities, and the blood of Jesus can turn a negative heart into a positive power for God and His kingdom. Glory to God forevermore!

Now let me say one thing before we move on. Unbelief is a sin. It is the major sin that can keep people out of heaven. It is the one that grieves the heart of God, relating to His own children. Have you ever had your children attack your integrity when you have always acted uprightly with them? It is very hurtful when they refuse to hear your heart. God is the perfect Father. He has never hurt us, let us down, or failed to be there for us, yet we act and talk like He has. He simply wants us to trust Him and believe the Word He has spoken to us. That is not all that unreasonable, is it? We need to believe and live in the realm of what God can do and leave unbelief behind.

We must understand and thoroughly grasp the truth that God wants us free. I am often amazed by the fact that to many people that idea is so foreign. I have thought about this many times—it must be terribly hard trying to serve God when you believe that He is the One who has caused all of your trouble. What is so disturbing to me is the number of *His own people* who believe that He is at the root of their problems. God is not our trouble. Let me say it again—God is not our trouble. He never has been and never will be! God really does want us to be free. That is why He sent Jesus to us. Think about it. We were already in eternal bondage through sin; already destined for destruction. God did not need to send Jesus to be our Deliverer if He wanted us to remain in bondage.

Our chains of bondage are not the result of the hand of God. If we are experiencing any type of bondage keeping us from victory, it is not God's doing or His will for our lives. It is the result of ignorance and unbelief concerning what the blood of Jesus can do in our lives. It is absolutely crucial that we look at the Word and understand the power of the blood of Jesus.

Some of us think we have things so terribly wrong with us that the blood cannot even reach us, much less change what is wrong in our lives. We have believed lies Satan has told us about ourselves. We have bought into those lies and accepted them as truth, then we have pulled away from God in shame.

Satan is a liar and a loser. Do not ever accept the lies he throws your way. I know that may be easier said than done, but we are going to get into the Bible and accept what *it* says. I will say it again—there are no impossible situations with God. He yearns to lift us up and give us victory over every obstacle in life. Praise God!

Oh, I know bad things come our way. Every one of us has difficulties and face potentially despairing circumstances, and those circumstances try to grab us and wrestle us down. But they cannot do it—they do not have the power to do it *unless we let them* take hold of us and gain control. Too often, we let a situation rule our lives. It is time for us to take a stand of authority in the name of Jesus. It is high time we rule the situation by His authority and see the power of God excel on our behalf.

We must take heed of that warning; we cannot afford to have a heart filled with unbelief or even the prospect of falling away from God. You and I both have tried to change our own hearts. If we could have changed the hearts of others, we would have done it years ago, right?

For whatever reason, it is very liberating for me to know I cannot change my heart. I have been in battles—big battles—heart-versus-flesh battles. I truly loved God, but I still struggled. I wanted to serve God, but I would find myself pulling away from God. I didn't want to pray or read God's wonderful Word, and sometimes I even wanted to call the church and tell them I would not be there. Then it dawned on me—I was the preacher. I had to be there.

I do not remember a time after my new birth that I just sat up at night and planned a way to walk away from Him. I do not ever remember writing out some kind of plan for how I was going to get back into sin. I just slowly, but surely, got away from the things of God—just got sidetracked. Unfortunately, once we get on that slippery slope leading us away from God, it is easy to just keep sliding.

Satan is a deceiver. He never tricks us head on. He always attacks from the rear. If we are not ever watchful to walk with God, or if we are not tuned in to the Spirit of God, we can very easily be deceived. Once deceived, our heart will begin to turn from God.

Let me make sure you understand. Having an impure or evil heart does not make us evil people. Every time we are outside of faith, we are in unbelief and could therefore be considered to have an "evil" or unregenerate heart.

The medical field is an area of concern here. We thank God for the medical profession and the wisdom that they have to help us. But a lot of times, they call us "terminal," and God's Word emphatically states that we are healed. When we believe the doctor's word more than we believe what God has said in His Word, we are out of line. I want to make sure we understand that our minds have a tendency to say to us, "I am not evil. I love God." I am not talking about an evil act here, but a heart, meaning our mind and thoughts, which is going contrary to the Word and will of God. We get into this arena when we are not trusting God.

Any distraction that comes our way, trying to get us

to follow after something other than God's Word, has the potential to lead us away from God and into trouble if we are not careful. God's Word must be our final authority, no matter what else we may hear. You know, we only see symptoms and circumstances, but God knows the root of our problem and how to deal with it. When we get distracted and off course from God's pathways of wisdom, His Word, one thing usually leads to another and we find ourselves disoriented, confused, and many times discouraged because we lose hope. We need God to empower us to live victoriously in this crazy world. Quite often though, even after we repent, we still have trouble getting back to our former spiritual level. Let's find out why.

three

Feeling Dirty?

And when he had called all the people unto him, he said unto them, "Hearken unto me every one of you, and understand: There is nothing from without a man, that entering into him can defile him: but the things which come out of him, those are they that defile the man. If any man have ears to hear, let him hear." And when he was entered into the house from the people, his disciples asked him concerning the parable. And he saith unto them, "Are ye so without understanding also? Do ye not perceive, that whatsoever thing from without entereth into the man, it cannot defile him; Because it entereth not into his heart, but into the belly, and goeth out into the draught, purging all meats?" And he said, "That which cometh out of the man, that defileth the man. For from within, out of the heart of men, proceed evil thoughts, adulteries, fornications, murders, Thefts, covetousness, wickedness, deceit, lasciviousness, an evil eye, blasphemy, pride, foolishness: All these evil things come from within, and defile the man."

—MARK 7:14–23

As I STUDIED THESE VERSES, my question was: What is meant by the word *defile*? I found out that there are approximately sixteen Greek and Hebrew words that are translated "defile," but we are going to focus on the four most common ones through various scripture passages, and show what they have to do with the cleansing power of the blood of Jesus.

One of those four words is found in this passage from the Book of Mark. The Greek translation for the word *defile* in these verses means "to make common." Sinful behavior, such as covetousness, deceit, and pride, are things that defile us and make us common. The truth of the matter is that we are not common. We are to walk uprightly—unlike mere men—because we are made in the image of God. When we participate in those sinful things of the world, we *become* common. When we become common, we are no longer godly. It is impossible to be godly and common at the same time. Now hear me, if we have participated in those activities to any degree, we can be totally forgiven and not yet totally cleansed.

But hang on, now. I am not coming against the blood of Jesus in any way. In the eyes of God, we are completely forgiven at the spirit level, but the residue of that sin hangs on in our heart, meaning our soulish area. I thought the heart and the spirit were one and the same for the longest time. But after long study, I discovered that is not necessarily true in every incident. We will get into that later.

When we walk in pride or walk in foolishness, we are walking like a common, unregenerate person. Let me put it another way. We are walking like a common, defiled man when we, for example, participate in evil thoughts. If we keep our mind on those evil thoughts, those thoughts will eventually get down into our heart. We are not talking about the crazy thoughts that sweep through our minds—those wild things that hit our conscious thinking and make us ask ourselves, *Where did that come from?* I am talking about those evil thoughts that we dwell on, focus on, and do not cast down as the Bible says we are supposed to.

How do we have these evil thoughts? Well, it can occur when we start thinking about somebody else's husband or wife in an ungodly manner, or dwell on thoughts of doing harm to another. Those are pretty obvious, aren't they? Let's get down to a more subtle area. Do we rejoice when harm comes to someone who has hurt us, thinking it just serves them right? Come on, now. When we behave like that, we are common, no different than the world. We are not to rejoice when anything harmful or evil comes against any person. Read 1 Corinthians 13. We can all look at fornication, murders, the thefts, and know that all those actions are wrong. Ah, but what about thoughts like, *Why doesn't Pastor ever let me sing?* Or, *Why doesn't he let me teach? Why doesn't Pastor realize I have the ability? I could do a better job than so and so.* My friend, that is the beginning of covetousness, which starts with an evil thought. What about all of those evil, hateful, or haughty looks? Some of us really have an evil eye. I mean, some people may not say a word, but just their look is enough to kill you. *Lord Jesus, help us.*

I love to watch people during our prayer times because it is a good time to see how people react. Everyone is on different spiritual levels. I know that. I do not get upset if somebody prays something that might not be quite on target. I am just glad they are praying. I agree with what is right, and I disagree with what is wrong, but I do not faint and fall on the floor when someone prays in error. We need to remember, we all have prayed like that in times past. Let's get honest, shall we? Once we are born again, we have to learn how to pray accurately, and that takes time. It bothers me when we get to a self-appointed place where we judge others with our little motions and our little doings like rolling our eyes in disgust or ridicule because others are not on our spiritual level. God never appointed any of us to sit on the judge's bench. We might as well just say, "Amen," my brothers and sisters. We are not to be or act common, but to undergird and help each other grow up in the things of the Lord.

Come on, church. We did not wake up one morning a spiritual giant. None of us are there yet, I assure you. But we are on our way, hallelujah. Sin defiles us because we are not reflecting the image of God that is within us.

Now, let's look at another scripture about defilement:

> Behold, the LORD's hand is not shortened, that it cannot save; neither his ear heavy, that it cannot hear: But your iniquities have separated between you and your God, and your sins have hid his face from you, that he will not hear. For your hands are defiled with blood, and your fingers with iniquity; your lips have spoken lies, your tongue hath muttered perverseness.
>
> —ISAIAH 59:1–3

The word *defiled* is translated here to mean "stained." So defilement in any way makes us common and stains us. Sin always leaves a stain. Now hear me carefully. *Repentance* does not mean "remove the stain," because repentance is simply changing direction. Repentance is when we quit heading in one direction, make an about face, and head in the opposite direction. But we can be going one way in sin, stop, and begin going another way, and yet the stain of that sin remains within us. That is what has been wrong with a lot of us. We have repented and repented and repented for the same thing, and we were forgiven by our gracious heavenly Father the very first time we confessed it. Yet, the stain of that sin has been the culprit that has made us feel like we were clothed in shame.

Oh yes, there is a way to remove that stain, but repentance does not *automatically* remove the stain. This should help us to understand what has happened to us in days past and why we feel the way we do. And with the help of the Lord Jesus Christ, we are going to learn how to walk forever free of those stains. Glory to God! He is so merciful to us. His divine provision is beyond our wildest dreams, and His love is stronger than our deepest sin.

Let's take a look at the Book of Genesis:

> And when Shechem the son of Hamor the Hivite, prince of the country, saw her, he took her, and lay with her, and defiled her.
>
> —Genesis 34:2

Defiled here means "to force to submit to uncleanness or to make one dirty." Let's recap: defilement makes us common, causes stains, and makes us dirty. We absolutely can be covered with "spiritual" dirt. That is why we need the blood of Jesus cleansing us continually:

> Behold, therefore I will bring strangers upon thee, the terrible of the nations: and they shall draw their swords against the beauty of thy wisdom, and they shall defile thy brightness.
>
> —Ezekiel 28:7

In this instance the word *defile* means "to wound, such as to lay open, give access to, or to cut something open." When we become defiled by sin, there is a wound that appears—not just a bruise, but an open wound within us. Let's recall that natural things teach us spiritual truths. Jesus often used the natural realm to explain heavenly principles. If our body has an open wound and it gets dirty, what happens to it? It gets infected, doesn't it? "He that hath an ear, let him hear" (Rev. 2:17). Infection sets in. Now, when we repent and change directions, we still can have an open wound or a spiritual infection from that sin deep within us which needs tending. If we do not stay under the teaching of sound doctrine, are not undergirded by our brothers and sisters in the Lord, or do not allow time for healing and cleansing to take place, we regress and fall back into our former behaviors. We are critically vulnerable if we do not let God take care of that wound, and cleanse it with the blood of the Lamb.

Sin is such a treacherous thing, and this stain of sin is just as serious. Too many of God's people have thought they can live however they want and not only make it to heaven, but walk in God's fullness day to day just because they once made a confession of faith to a pastor long ago. It is impossible to walk uprightly, manifesting the glory of the Lord, while remaining defiled. We may have wondrous mountain-top experiences; we may fly like an eagle up there, but then crash land like a turkey.

It has happened to all of us at one time or another. Thank God, He has made provision for us to be overcomers and walk in victory daily. Glory to God! He has laid a path for it, and given us the instruction and the power to do it. I am telling you, church, we are going to do this thing; we can walk in victory, and we are going to do it right. The glorious church will rise above this thing to the glory of God the Father, and show this dying world the goodness of Jehovah, the King of the universe. Somebody needs to say *Amen*, because this is good news to discover the provision God has made for us to walk free. I know because I have felt wounded; I have felt stained; I have felt dirty; and I have certainly felt common. This is shouting ground! Oh, I am so glad that the residue, the stain of any sin, can be washed away by the blood of Jesus. Hallelujah!

A noted and very anointed evangelist, credited with preaching that has literally brought millions of people into the kingdom of God, has said that in their follow-up efforts, his ministry is not able to find the majority of the people who came down to get saved during his meetings. They repented all right, but there was still something there that has greatly hindered them. They did not get into a church or move forward with God. All of us need to be admonished to give God our whole life, get in a good church that preaches the full gospel, and be consistent there so we can be healed of all this mess that is within us. If we dedicate ourselves to God in such a manner, we can walk in victory. But if we bounce in and out, and come and go at our convenience, we will get sidetracked. If we do not stay centered on God's Word and His principles, we are going to get lost in the shuffle and remain wounded. We will find ourselves resentful of others, especially those who have remained faithful and are now way ahead of us spiritually. Watch out if you start saying, "I don't want to go to church. I don't believe I have to be at church all the time…blah, blah, blah." When you hear yourself saying such things, you can know you are moving backwards, not forward with God.

People who say those kinds of things will not walk in

victory. Because they do not know what else to do, they will lash out at you. When they see changes in your life—how you are excelling, how things seem to be going well for you—and because they are not willing to do those same things, they will begin to talk, saying hurtful, negative things.

There are certain spiritual things in our lives that must be tended daily, and most of them must be tended over a period of time to be fully restored. We have to *stick with the program* to walk in victory. It takes time to work things out that are deep within us. If everyone who has ever come down to the altar in our church and repented were still attending our services, we would have to meet at the downtown stadium. We are unable to keep up with them; they just come and go, come and go. We have to dedicate ourselves to a new lifestyle, and Jesus will be there to see that we are victorious. Glory to God!

This is a one-sided fight, but not enough of us seem to know it. God is always on our side. It gives Him great pleasure when He sees us put the devil under our feet. It is God's great pleasure to give us the kingdom. Hallelujah!

> Ah sinful nation, a people laden with iniquity, a seed of evildoers, children that are corrupters: they have forsaken the LORD, they have provoked the Holy One of Israel unto anger, they are gone away backward. Why should ye be stricken any more? ye will revolt more and more: the whole head is sick, and the whole heart faint. From the sole of the foot even unto the head there is no soundness in it; but wounds, and bruises, and putrifying sores: they have not been closed, neither bound up, neither mollified with ointment.
>
> —ISAIAH 1:4–6

Feeling Dirty?

This is a picture of what the church looks like when it is laden with sin. Keep in mind the fact that this passage of Scripture is talking about God's people, the ones who are supposed to know better. Oh yes, there are defilements present within the church, and we have not given them time for their healing to occur.

> To what purpose is the multitude of your sacrifices unto me? saith the LORD: I am full of the burnt offerings of rams, and the fat of fed beasts; and I delight not in the blood of bullocks, or of lambs, or of he goats....Wash you, make you clean; put away the evil of your doings from before mine eyes; cease to do evil.
>
> —ISAIAH 1:11, 16

The key to turning all of these situations around is the washing. Whether we are dirty, wounded, common, or stained, we need a good washing—not just a good cover-up, but a thorough washing. We need something that is really going to take that mess, that defilement, away from us. Let me tell you, washing is not a one-time experience; not in the natural or in the spiritual realms. Regrettably, there have been many who have tried that, but we can always smell them coming. Washing must be done on a continuous basis in both the natural and the spiritual.

There are some good passages in the Bible about washing. Let me share just a few of them with you:

> Have mercy upon me, O God, according to thy lovingkindness: according unto the multitude of thy tender mercies blot out my transgressions. Wash me thoroughly from mine iniquity, and cleanse me from my sin.
>
> —PSALM 51:1–2

29

Behold, I will bring it health and cure, and I will cure them, and will reveal unto them the abundance of peace and truth. And I will cause the captivity of Judah and the captivity of Israel to return, and will build them, as at the first. And I will cleanse them from all their iniquity, whereby they have sinned against me; and I will pardon all their iniquities, whereby they have sinned, and whereby they have transgressed against me. And it shall be to me a name of joy, a praise and an honour before all the nations of the earth, which shall hear all the good that I do unto them: and they shall fear and tremble for all the goodness and for all the prosperity that I procure unto it.

—JEREMIAH 33:6–9

Husbands, love your wives, even as Christ also loved the church, and gave himself for it; That he might sanctify and cleanse it with the washing of water by the word, That he might present it to himself a glorious church, not having spot, or wrinkle, or any such thing; but that it should be holy and without blemish.

—EPHESIANS 5:25–27

John to the seven churches which are in Asia: Grace be unto you, and peace, from him which is, and which was, and which is to come; and from the seven Spirits which are before his throne; And from Jesus Christ, who is the faithful witness, and the first begotten of the dead, and the prince of the kings of the earth. Unto him that loved us, and washed us from our sins in his own blood, And hath made us kings and priests unto God and his Father; to him be glory and dominion for ever and ever. Amen.

—REVELATION 1:4–6

Now, let's look at 1 John:

> But if we walk in the light, as he is in the light, we
> have fellowship one with another, and the blood of
> Jesus Christ his Son cleanseth us from all sin. If we say
> that we have no sin, we deceive ourselves, and the truth
> is not in us.
>
> —1 JOHN 1:7–8

Look at the word *cleanseth* in verse 7. Interestingly, it de-
notes a continuous cleansing as we walk in the light of His
Word and by the blood of Jesus. I believe that is the loop-
hole with which Satan has deceived the church. We are to be
cleansed daily by the blood of the Lamb, yet we have thought
this cleansing needed to occur only at the moment of our new
birth and then that was it.

I was raised Baptist. I cherish my Baptist background,
and my ordination papers are still with the Baptist church.
As I grew up and experienced life and failure, I got "saved"
many times. I know we can only get saved once, but I felt
unclean and stained by my shortcomings, even after repenting. I simply did not know what else to do.

Can you identify with this struggle to be free? I repeat-
edly asked the Lord to come back into my heart, hoping to
experience the same freedom as when I first got saved. The
truth is, I did not need to get saved again because Jesus
never actually left me; neither will He leave you. How many
of us have crawled to the altar, sobbing our hearts out, beg-
ging for forgiveness, and trying to get saved again and be
restored to God?

The truth is, we get tainted in life by what occurs around
us. We all continue to miss the mark of excellence set by

God's standards. Knowing that God does not flow through dirty vessels, is it any wonder that when we go and lay hands on the sick, nothing happens? I am going to share with you something I believe you will shout about: we are going to learn how to wash ourselves in the blood of the Lamb as priests, and walk free and clean of every defilement. Praise God forevermore! Stay with me. It gets better.

four

Fulfilling the Law

*Think not that I am come to destroy the law, or
the prophets: I am not come to destroy, but to fulfil.*

—MATTHEW 5:17

JESUS IS THE FULFILLMENT OF the law; that is certainly the
truth. As born-again, children of God, we know this truth,
don't we? In this age of grace, we like to shout, "I am not under
the law," but the law is really not a bad thing. It describes
a lifestyle that is pleasing to God, but seemingly tough to
keep. The problem I see in the church is that we have been
ignorant of what Jesus fulfilled for us. We need to know what
He fulfilled so we can walk in every blessing—or His work is
useless to us.

Hosea 4:6 says that God's people are destroyed for a
lack of knowledge. We are not required to live under the letter of the law because Jesus fulfilled the law. We will not
be held under its bondage of rules and regulations. We are

grateful we do not have that obligation because old covenant saints had difficulty fully keeping it.

However, the spirit of the law is different. It is hugely advantageous for us to have a working knowledge of its principles, just as we would from any other old covenant passages such as ones found in Isaiah, Proverbs, or the Psalms. As New Testament saints, we live and move and have our being mainly in the epistles, but that does not negate the truths dispersed throughout the rest of the Bible. The New Testament simply completes and explains the old. Although Jesus fulfilled the law two thousand years ago, we are certainly involved in its fulfillment today through Him. Can we grasp what a privilege it is to be involved in the work of God on Earth? When we know what belongs to us, we can shout from the housetops, "Thank God. Jesus fulfilled the law for me. Glory to His name!"

Thank You, dear Jesus. Because of Your mighty work, I take great pride in walking in the fulfillment of the law. Hallelujah!

Obviously though, if we do not know what God did for us through our Lord Jesus, we are just rattling when we are up against the devil. To look the devil square in the face with boldness, and tell him in no uncertain terms that we are free of sin and that we will not take the burden or shame of it again, requires knowledge of the law and what Jesus has fulfilled. It makes a notable difference how we respond to life's situations when we have a clear understanding of the provisions of Calvary. Although God writes His commandments on the tablets of our heart, we still need to be familiar with the law.

For instance, we need to know that the Jewish holy days were set down by the law. These days are called the feasts of the Lord. (See Lev. 23:2.) Here is a question: Whose feasts are they? God instructed the Jewish people to celebrate these festivals, but obviously they were God's feasts because they were known as the feasts of the Lord. It becomes extremely interesting when we look up two particular Hebrew words in this verse. The first is one that is translated *feast*. One of its main meanings is appointment. The other word is *convocations*. It means an assembly, but it also means a rehearsal. Could it be that these feast days are God's appointed times to do something specific while He commands the Jewish people to celebrate or rehearse them yearly? That revelation by itself is an eye-opener knowing that God has appointments He will accomplish on a certain day at a certain time. I tell you again, Jesus fulfilled the law, and He fulfilled the required spring festivals of Passover, the Feast of Unleavened Bread, the Feast of First Fruits, and Pentecost—to the day and hour as set down in the law. Glory to God!

The spring festivals set the precedence, and undoubtedly in time, the fall festivals will be fulfilled also. The next one to be fulfilled is the Feast of the Blowing of the Trumpet (the shofar). We all know what happens when the trumpet is blown, don't we? Glory to God and hallelujah! The Feast of Tabernacles is another that has yet to be fulfilled in God's appointment book, when God literally comes down and tabernacles with His people. But, it is coming, according to the law. We know it will happen during the millennial kingdom, but the Jewish people celebrate it every year according to the law.

We Gentiles have observed some of the holy days and not others. Just the same, God gave *all* of them in the law.

We are not under the law, or required to obey all of the rituals of the feasts, but if these holy days give us a "calendar" for coming events, wouldn't it behoove us to be at least familiar with it? God's Word is full of nuggets of wisdom of His plan for the coming days. Praise God forever!

Then, there is a part of the law that we are concentrating on in this book. Let's take a look at it:

> Now this is that which thou shalt offer upon the altar; two lambs of the first year day by day *continually*. The one lamb thou shalt offer in the morning; and the other lamb thou shalt offer at even.
>
> —EXODUS 29:38–39, emphasis added

Here is one sacrifice that God said does not stop. As a matter of fact, if we read Jewish history, we would discover that there was an attempt to stop this particular sacrifice during Daniel's time, and it was successfully halted at the end of the Roman season. Hebrew historians state that when Babylon forced Israel to stop these morning and evening sacrifices, the greatest devastations, the greatest impacts, occurred.

Check out the word *continually*. It means perpetually, or that which shall never cease. Under the old covenant, this event was called the morning and evening sacrifice, and it happened each and every day. Priests had to wash in the blood morning and evening. Jesus fulfilled this part of the law too, and is *still fulfilling* it today in the spirit dimension! For us, the Lamb was slain at Calvary's cross; there is no further need for sacrifices. But today, He is still our morning and evening sacrifice in the spirit realm. How do we partake of this sacrifice? By applying His blood to our lives each day with the words of our confession, morning and evening, because the Old Testament sacrifice was that of blood. If the blood of sacrificial animals was able to accomplish what it did as a type and symbol of the Lamb that was to come, how much more is the living blood of Jesus able to accomplish this cleansing for us today?

Are you with me? If you and I are not daily applying the blood, we are walking around defiled, common, stained, and wounded. Today, we walk out in the Spirit what they did in the natural under the old covenant. When we walk around defiled, we experience a "power shortage" in our lives because God needs to work through clean vessels. Truly, we have not understood the power in the blood of Jesus that belongs to us and what it can accomplish. Hear it again. It was required for priests to wash daily. We are going to find out that we are priests unto God in Christ Jesus our Lord, and that we can and should be operating in that office as a born-again child of God. We will be absolutely amazed at our responsibilities and privileges.

> If we say that we have fellowship with him, and walk in darkness, we lie, and do not the truth: But if we walk in the light, as he is in the light, we have fellowship one with another, and the blood of Jesus Christ his Son cleanseth us from all sin.
>
> —1 JOHN 1:6–7

That word *cleanseth* means that it is not a one-time happening, but an ongoing process. There is to be a continuous cleansing by the blood of the Lamb in our lives. Just as we take daily baths in the natural, we are to be cleansed from contaminants by the blood of the Lamb in the spirit dimension. Jesus fulfilled the law. He did not wipe it out. Today, we partake of it freely, not under the letter of the law, but under the Spirit of the law. Thank You, Jesus.

Most of us are carrying around a lot of baggage that holds us back from being the glorious church He foreordained us to be. We are stained, common, dirty, and wounded. It could have been a wound that took place twenty years ago, but we are still carrying it around with us. We have probably learned how to cover it up and hide it from others, but it continues to hang unmercifully around our neck and come up at us in the night hours. We find ourselves in our quiet time, endeavoring to praise God in spirit and truth, when there it is again, slapping us in the face. Even the emotions resurrect, and again we cower before our God in disgrace and shame. What do we do? We repent again as tears stream down our face over a sin long ago forgiven and cleansed by the blood of the Lamb. We will repent long enough to start feeling all right again. Many of us have been there. It is so true for all of us because we have not understood what Jesus has done for us. We are to wash ourselves in the blood of the Lamb, morning and evening. We are to wash ourselves and give Him praise because the mighty blood of the Lamb conquers the stain and heals the wound. Praise His Holy name forever! He is so wonderful!

There is nothing in our lives that the blood of Jesus Christ has not already conquered. It does not matter what our problem is or what situation we may be facing. The answer is emphatically the blood of Jesus. It is the strongest power in the world. While working hand in glove with the exchanges at Calvary and the name of the Lord Jesus, this Trio will get the job done—and done right.

In the same light, there are those who would say, "I haven't committed any sin, and I do not need cleansing."

I hope sin is not a part of our lifestyle before God and others, but we are not as holy as we think we are. Look at the world in which we live. We live in a cesspool. This world is full of corruption and defilements. Daily we are bombarded by its degradations. In the same way, we do not necessarily have to have had a romp in the mud to take a bath in the natural. Our day could have been spent in an office building where there was no dirt pile, but still we take a bath because we feel dirty just from this environment, the fallen world. Are you with me? Look at this:

> Pure religion and undefiled before God and the Father is this, To visit the fatherless and widows in their affliction, and to keep himself unspotted from the world.
>
> —JAMES 1:27

Notice, it did not say to keep ourselves unspotted from sin. It directed us to keep ourselves unspotted from the world. Look at it again. I was amazed when I saw that. I looked up the word *world* and found out it refers to the influence from the world's systems and its ungodly multitudes. We are to keep ourselves from the evil influences of the world, because being in this world will contaminate us and deposit filth upon us. We are to keep ourselves cleansed and unspotted from the influences of the world and its ungodliness. That which is ungodly around us, corrupts us.

Here is another verse saying the same thing. This is part of Jesus' prayer in the Garden of Gethsemane to the Father before His crucifixion, and the Bible uses the very same word:

> I pray not that thou shouldest take them out of the
> world, but that thou shouldest keep them from the
> evil.
>
> —John 17:15

The word *evil* here means two things in the New Testament. One is the act that we do. The other is the influence of an ungodly, corrupting world (not an act of sin). Jesus prayed that God would keep us from the ungodly influence of the world, not just take us out of it. We need to be the lights in the midst of this dark world. The world we live in, my friend, is a mess—a cesspool of evil contaminants that will attach themselves to us should we allow it. We need to wash and cleanse ourselves of these things. We can do it. Jesus has already helped us. He prayed that God would help us to stay clean from the evil influences of the world in which we live. Surely, His prayers were heard and answered, don't you think?

There are only two things identified in the Bible that will wash us: the Word and the blood. Most of us have learned over the years how to get into the Word and be washed with the water of the Word. But I do not think we know how to wash, or how to apply the blood every day. I don't think the church as a whole has had the understanding of the importance of the morning and evening cleansing by the precious blood of the Lord Jesus. Oh, we sing about the blood all right, but I am talking about making the power of the blood work in our lives. The power in our life comes from our ability to apply the Word of God combined with the relationship we have with Jesus Christ. Yet, the application of the blood is the source of our cleansing to do such things.

We are born again, but are we clean? The power we exhibit in our lives depends on our relationship with Jesus and how clean we are. The evil influence of the world will taint us and make us unclean for the ministry that God has called us to accomplish. Among other things, our ears, mouth, hands, and eyes must be cleansed by the blood daily. We must learn to be clean vessels for the days ahead. We cannot just flip-flop from dirty to clean when the notion strikes us. Many come to church cursing their spouse in the car, then walk into church and say, "Hallelujah," and still think everything is all right with God simply because they changed faces walking in the door. Then they leave after the service and talk about how much God was in that service. That, my friend, is a sad joke. All they have had is some fleshly moment, not an experience with God, because God is holy and His true presence brings conviction of ungodly behavior.

God pointed out that very thing to me about my own life. He identified all of the wasted preaching and teaching I did over the years under the pretense that He was in it. He revealed the many times that I stood before His people to preach and I had not been walking uprightly before Him. I believed there was a move of God and that something was happening among the people. His Word did not return unto Him void, but most assuredly, the meeting was not as it should have been. Those of us who have a call on our lives, whether in the fivefold ministry, or whether we teach, preach, play an instrument, or usher at the door, we must get the junk out and just live right all the time by the power of the Holy Spirit. Most of us believe like I did and think that we can just say, "God forgive me," but with no change of behavior, we will be clean and holy. Wrong! We have to learn to live, not only tighter with God, but learn how to apply the blood of Jesus as a bath.

We cannot live like the devil, cussing and carrying on,

tearing people's lives up with our mouths, and then plead, "Forgive me, Jesus," and think that little "so-called" repentance is a stamp of approval from God. Certainly, all of us have done just that in one way or another. We must bow before Him, repent (earnestly change directions) with all of our heart, and receive our cleansing. I am talking about our *holy* God, not Joe Blow down the street. I am talking about Jehovah, the Creator of heaven and Earth. We are talking about the God of eternity, who has cherubim and angels around Him who say nothing but "Holy, holy, holy." Then we come be-bopping into the church service after living a sloppy, carnal life all week, lift our hands toward heaven, and think we have entered into the presence of God. We have not, my brothers and sisters. I tell you, it would be grim for us if it were not for the provisions of God and the blood of Jesus. Thank God for His mercy toward us.

When this truth came as revelation to me, I publicly asked God to forgive me, and asked the people to forgive me for the times I preached or laid hands on them and did not fully understand the seriousness of my actions. I was ignorant—just absolutely ignorant. He has been so gracious to me.

We are talking about life and death issues here. We are talking about a God who is calling us to Himself, so that our hands can be an expression of Him and His everlasting love to others. The Bible does not say that the New Testament saints extended their hands. It says they extended *His* hands. The glorious church is to be like Him. We were created to think like Him, to walk like Him, and talk like Him through the provision of the life-changing blood of the Lamb. If we will learn to bathe in it, we can experience a cleansing beyond our wildest dreams. The blood will break the power of that thing we have been dragging around. Certainly, repentance is the first step, but then we need to go further and bathe ourselves in the blood and watch what will happen. Oh, how we need to appreciate and honor His precious blood! The blood flows from Immanuel's veins to remove the stains, the wounds, the dirt, and the commonness and make us whole to the glory of God the Father. Thank You, Jesus. You are so wonderful.

We are to keep Jesus vibrant in our hearts, and allow Him to take an active role and lead us step-by-step. Here is one danger we face. Although we are born again and have the Spirit of grace abiding in our heart, we allow our heart to leave Him first, and then our feet follow. The prodigal son left in his heart (soulish area—the mind, will, and emotions) before he ever took a physical step away from his home and father. The application of the blood is instrumental in maintaining an intimate relationship with God.

We have learned how to plead the blood of Jesus over our natural man for protection. We have done it for years. God is revealing to us now that there is another dimension that is available to us that Satan has blinded us from. We have pled the blood for safety, but the blood has to be applied for cleansing in the spirit realm. My Bible teaches me if my hands are not clean, God does not even hear me when I pray. I have to be clean, and He did not mean physical hands. We are talking about a heart issue. Now, let's talk about the heart and spirit of man.

five

What Is the
Heart Anyway?

WE HAVE TAUGHT FOR YEARS that the heart and the spirit are the same. There are a couple of instances in Scripture when they are used interchangeably. In fact, without doing a little bit of studying on this word, we would not know they were different in the first place. But I guarantee you, most of the time we see the word *heart* in Old Testament scriptures, it does not mean the "spirit" of a man. Let's take a look.

First of all, if we are born again, our spirit is the part of us that underwent the great transformation the moment we were born into God's family. Our spirit is then tuned toward Christ and to the things of God. He resides in our born-again spirit. Remember, this is a New Testament fulfillment for those who are born again. If the heart and the spirit are one and the same in all instances, especially in the Old Testament, how do we reconcile this belief with Scripture in Jeremiah as well as others?

> The heart is deceitful above all things, and desperately wicked: who can know it?

—Jeremiah 17:9

That is pretty hard, isn't it? To be honest, it sounds grim. For those folks who have not yet accepted Jesus as their Lord and Savior, that verse is true. But, once born again, I promise you, our spirit man is neither wicked nor deceitful. Before our new birth, our spirit is deaf to God's voice. Spiritually dead people do not long to live a lifestyle pleasing to Him. Why? Because He is not living inside of them, so their hearts are dark, full of sin, and desperately wicked. But the miraculous new birth changes all of that. We are justified and reconciled to Him, literally made in His image. Glory to God! Spirits made in the image of the Almighty are neither deceitful nor wicked.

We need to get in the Word to see what it actually says because we at times believe things that are not so. We must let the Word do the talking; in other words, keep it in context. Let me give you an example in the natural realm; sometimes it is easier to see spiritual truths there. If I were to ask you to give me the heart of a watermelon, it would be the center part, the best part, the part with no seeds. The heart is the center of the melon. In the same way, our heart is almost always—in the Old Testament and sometimes even in the New Testament—the center of our soulish area. The heart is the center of the intellect, the mind, and the emotions. If our spirit is God-indwelt and in right standing with Him, and our heart is the center of our spirit, how in the world can our heart be wicked? Never, ever is there a word spoken against the born-again spirit. Not so with the heart.

There are some pretty tough things said about the heart. Every attitude, every appetite, and every issue of our life will be interpreted through the soulish area, meaning the heart in most instances. That is why we must renew our minds and save our souls by the Word of God. Scripture states that out of a good heart, good things come to pass, and out of a bad heart, bad things come to pass. The heart and the spirit cannot be one and the same in all instances. Our born-again spirit is after God. It is clean and pure. That is where the Holy Spirit resides, inside our born-again spirit. Do you want to tell me that the heart of our spirit is deceptive? I don't think so! Think about it.

Keep in mind that we are not talking about the physical heart that pumps blood throughout our body. That is where people got so confused when doctors began performing heart transplants years ago. Boy, did we hear some wild tales. "Sally is not Sally anymore, because she has Sue's heart," you were likely to hear. How does Sally know what she is thinking? It could be one of Sue's thoughts. What if Sue loved Tom, and Sally is married to Dick? Who is Dick married to now? Listen, we laugh now, but major controversy in theological circles erupted from such questions. I am telling you, we were dumb and dumber—Jesus help us.

> Keep thy heart with all diligence; for out of it are the issues of life.
>
> —PROVERBS 4:23

That is not to say, "Do not have a heart transplant." I am going to show you how protecting our hearts, and renewing our hearts and minds are hitting at the same thing. As a man thinks in his heart, so is he. (See Prov. 23:7.) In other words, if a man (or woman) thinks a certain way, that is the way that man really is. Well, what part does thinking come from? It comes from the mind, in the soulish part of our being. The heart does think, and many of our thought processes take place in the heart. Every action we perform outwardly is a result of our heart (soulish area) and its condition. That is bad news if our heart has problems.

We are made up of three components—spirit, soul, and body. We are a spirit, we have a soul, and we live in a body. When we die, we leave the body, but we are still alive. Our spirit is of God, born of God, and made in the image of God. Our soul is our mind, will, and emotions. That is the part of us we are instructed to renew by the Word of God. If we desire to think God's thoughts, we have to learn to think differently. That process is called renewing the mind. The Bible says that the Word of God is able to save the soul and make it line up with the Word of God. This is so we can walk in victory in our soulish area and allow our spirit to get in agreement with the Word of God, thus conquering the flesh, which is always at enmity with the spirit.

Many times, when the Bible speaks of the heart, it is talking about the soulish area. Let's look at some scriptures that refer to this:

> Thou shalt also consider in thine heart, that, as a man chasteneth his son, so the LORD thy God chasteneth thee.
>
> —DEUTERONOMY 8:5

> And it came to pass, as she continued praying before the LORD, that Eli marked her mouth. Now Hannah, she spake in her heart; only her lips moved, but her voice was not heard: therefore Eli thought she had been drunken.
>
> —1 SAMUEL 1:12–13

Let the words of my mouth, and the meditation of my heart, be acceptable in thy sight, O Lord, my strength, and my redeemer.

—Psalm 19:14

For verily I say unto you, That whosoever shall say unto this mountain, Be thou removed, and be thou cast into the sea; and shall not doubt in his heart, but shall believe that those things which he saith shall come to pass; he shall have whatsoever he saith.

—Mark 11:23

And immediately when Jesus perceived in his spirit that they so reasoned within themselves, he said unto them, "Why reason ye these things in your hearts?"

—Mark 2:8

Thy word have I hid in mine heart, that I might not sin against thee.

—Psalm 119:11

Let them not depart from thine eyes; keep them in the midst of thine heart.

—Proverbs 4:21

But Mary kept all these things, and pondered them in her heart.

—Luke 2:19

That if thou shalt confess with thy mouth the Lord Jesus, and shalt believe in thine heart that God hath raised him from the dead, thou shalt be saved.

—Romans 10:9

That was just a few of the heart- and soul-related passages, but here are some more: Exodus 4:14; Exodus 4:21; Deuteronomy 6:5; 1 Chronicles 22:19; 2 Chronicles 6:7; Psalm 119:36; Proverbs 12:25; Isaiah 57:15; Luke 24:32; John 14:1; and Romans 10:1.

An impure heart can corrupt our thoughts, not to mention our feelings, our words, and our actions. What I am saying can change our lives forever. We have to get this. Then I can tell you how to apply the blood of Jesus as a priest to those who have walked away from God and then watch God work in their lives.

As a priest of God, we all have a right to apply the blood to certain situations and certain people, especially those in our household or family. Here is what I am saying: we can apply the blood to somebody's heart (in the spirit realm) and affect their mind, their will, and their emotions. By letting the blood of Jesus in, to flow through and upon them, we can break away the blinders from their soulish eyes so they can have clearer vision and understanding of the things of God. We may have some disagreement about dealing with the will of a person, but I want you to think about something. There is no one in their right mind who chooses to go to hell. They are deceived and blinded; Satan has captured them against their will, meaning they did not deliberately choose hell for their lives and their eternal future.

None of us set out to end up in captivity. We walk on our path thinking we are making sound decisions for our lives. Before we came to the Lord, you and I both were held captive by deception and blindness as well. As other unregenerate people, our hearts were perverted toward God and His ways of living uprightly. After our new birth and after some learning and understanding of the Word of God, we realize it is our choices that guide our lives. But there are multitudes who know nothing about God or how He desires to flood their lives with goodness. There are many who are absolutely drawn to sin. They cannot see sin the way God sees it because their eyes are blinded by the enemy of their soul.

When we talk about the heart, we are talking about that part of each of us that was not brought immediately under the redemption of the blood of Jesus. It does not obtain the benefits of this redemption until we apply the blood, do what Romans 12:1–2 talks about, and get about the renewing of our soulish areas with His Word so we can think the thoughts of God. Jeremiah 17:9 says that our hearts are so desperately wicked that no one can know it. He says our hearts are deceitful. Guess who it deceives? Us! We go around thinking how wonderful and good we are. Just about the time we think we have it together, we are deceived. Our spirit man can be righteous in the sight of God, but our heart can be wicked and deceitful. Could it be that every shortcoming and failure that you and I have had is a result of an area of our heart that has not been dealt with by the blood of Jesus? Yes, it could. Not because the blood of Jesus cannot soak into every crevice of our heart and cleanse us, but because the Lord will not impose Himself on us. He will not come in without an open invitation to all areas of our heart.

Think about someone you know who is born again, but not serving God. We are not talking about the lost now, but a member of the body of Christ. They came to the Lord Jesus, but we cannot find them now. They are not in church anywhere. They used to be on fire for the things of God, but now they are cold, and it seems as if their heart has hardened.

Their spirit is not hard, but their heart, their soul, is.

We all know folks who go around the same mountain a thousand times. Mamas and daddies are grieved about their children who have walked away from God. They are not praying or reading God's precious words of instruction. We can beg them to come back, or threaten them with the prospect of hell if they do not straighten up. We have tried everything we can think of, but these people just keep on running the other way as fast as they can, into all kinds of sin. We get torn up because they have not heard a word we have said. We cry, we intercede, we wonder what is going on. We cannot understand the problem, because we know they know better. Nothing seems to faze them. But there is something that God has already accomplished that will help us to set them free. Praise God forevermore. Thank Him for the blood of the Lamb.

> Blessed are the pure in heart: for they shall see God.
>
> —MATTHEW 5:8

> A good man out of the good treasure of the heart bringeth forth good things: and an evil man out of the evil treasure bringeth forth evil things.
>
> —MATTHEW 12:35

If the pure in heart will be the only ones to see God, then it seems to me that something needs to be done at the heart level. We are not going to change these people just by our prayers; we also have to deal with their heart. I remind you that the Bible says that the heart is desperately wicked. As a matter of fact, Scripture states that there is warfare at the heart level. The apostle Paul dealt with this very issue. He wanted to do one thing, but he ended up doing another. He wanted to do good, but found himself doing just the opposite. He basically said, "You know I really want to serve God and then there's this other side that does not want to serve Him at all" (Rom. 7:14–17, author's paraphrase).

I know what it's like to be saved and still be divided. How many of you are honest enough to admit that very same thing? I am telling you, it is a heart problem. But, thank God, there is hope for our hearts. I want to show you why that is, and then I want to show you what we can do about it as kings and priests unto God, walking in kingdom authority and living effectually for and in the kingdom of God. Hallelujah!

six

Washing the Highs and the Lows

IN THE LAST FEW CHAPTERS, I shared that the reason many times we fall back into trouble and fail to maintain victory after repenting is that we have not washed ourselves with the blood of the Lamb and allowed cleansing and healing to take place deep within us. It has been very common in the church to believe that once people are saved, they are OK and that is all there is. Many times, we stay with them until they accept the Lord Jesus, but then basically abandon them after that, thinking that because now they are saved, they are fine. Yet, we turn our nose up at their behavior as if some magical something will change their actions overnight.

Sadly, sometimes we have thought, *Get with the program guys. Get your act together.* We have failed to remember they are but babies in the kingdom of God. The saints have not taught them on the power of the blood of Jesus, nor have we nurtured them as babes. None of us were born a spiritual giant. We were all born as babies into the kingdom of God, ignorant of how it works. Without teaching, everyone stays an infant in spiritual things. We have been casting them out into a world that is devouring these little ones in Christ. We must give people time to be cleansed and healed. We must tell them about the power, authority, and victory available to them.

We are called to walk in His image, but when sin enters our lives, we become defiled. Amazingly, Jesus is coming back for a glorious, victorious church who overcomes the trials of life. Can we ever get there? We sure can. Jesus has paid for everything we need to walk in this glorious state. The provision of the blood is the powerhouse of God. The blood was the ransom, the price paid for eternal life. In fact, the higher life is where He wants us, so we have all the assistance of heaven. Life in Jesus is just too good. Hallelujah! Let's look at another Scripture passage:

> Then cometh he to Simon Peter: and Peter saith unto him, Lord, dost thou wash my feet? Jesus answered and said unto him, "What I do thou knowest not now; but thou shalt know hereafter." Peter saith unto him, Thou shalt never wash my feet. Jesus answered him, "If I wash thee not, thou hast no part with me." Simon Peter saith unto him, Lord, not my feet only, but also my hands and my head. Jesus saith to him, "He that is washed needeth not save to wash his feet, but is clean every whit: and ye are clean, but not all." For he knew who should betray him; therefore said he, "Ye are not all clean."
>
> —JOHN 13:6–11

Let's put this whole thing in perspective again. Remember that we are talking about how to get past those besetting sins and the constant yo-yo effect of being pulled and dragged by things we cannot seem to overcome. We haul these things around with us all of our lives, and then, in a moment of weakness, wham! They pull us down completely, and we find ourselves bottomed out in the pit. I have good news, though—this can be overcome. We can walk free of it through the blood of the Lord Jesus. That, my friend, is shouting ground. Those verses I just cited are not just scriptures on humility or the heart of a servant. There is more revelation to this than humility.

Jesus said, "Peter, you've already had your bath, but not all of you are clean" (John 13:10–11). Now let me ask you something. Who is Jesus talking about? Most of us would blurt out, "Oh, He is talking about Judas. He's the one who is not clean." Theologically, people agree that Judas is the one that He is talking about. But, if that is true, and He is talking about Judas here, why is Jesus washing Peter's feet? Why is He not washing Judas's feet? Jesus said Peter was clean, yet He was washing Peter's feet. Could Jesus possibly be saying that Peter had been defiled by being around Judas?

You see, all they needed was a little spot bath. Back in the country, we call it a "spit" bath. If you are not from the country, you probably do not have any idea what I am talking about. It is not a complete bath, just a little touchup where we hit the highs and lows. Jesus was simply saying to Peter, "I do not need to wash you all over, but there are certain places that need to be taken care of" (John 13:10–11).

The same is true for us, even today. We are already saved, already scrubbed in the blood of the Lamb, so we do not need another bath. But, everyday we become defiled by the evil world around us, and we have to wash certain things that have come in contact with that filth. There are natural areas that need constant, daily cleansing. But just as in the natural realm, there are spiritual things we should wash every day, because spiritual areas also need that same attention.

The same principle is found in Ephesians 6, when Paul starts talking about putting on the armor of God. He was not talking about throwing things on their heads and wrapping things around their bodies. They were not tying the Word of God on their hands or anything like that. The armor is spiritual, and it was a spiritual situation in that foot-washing Peter received from Jesus. Every area of our being needs cleansing by the blood of Jesus just as our natural body needs cleansing. I used the illustration that in the natural we are born once and must continue to wash the rest of our days. If the natural is a picture of the spirit world, why is it we get born again, and we think that's enough of the blood to last the rest of our days without constantly being aware of its power and application? Why haven't we continued to wash ourselves daily with the blood of Jesus?

There has been a power shortage in our lives because we have been dirty, wounded, common, and stained and have failed to apply the blood of the Lamb. Let's be honest. We have all pulled wrong people to our bosom. We have gone to bed with the dogs and have gotten up with fleas. We have embraced the world and people who have no desire for us to walk uprightly.

ﻉﻟ ﻉﻟ ﻉﻟ ﻉﻟ

There are certain areas that really need to be cleansed continually—particular areas that will determine whether we walk in victory or not. The mouth is one of them. When I was growing up and I said a dirty word, my mother had a way of dealing with it—with a bar of soap. You know what I am talking about, don't you? Well, our mouths can be defiled spiritually as well. We have all learned that the words of our mouths are extremely important. They literally are setting our destiny and the goals we will ultimately reach, either good or bad. We have to wake up, stop that mess, and align our words with the Word of God, because all that junk that oozes out of our mouths is causing defeat in our lives. We must quit running our mouth, playing games, and talking about things of the world with laughter when they are abominations before God.

Those who know me to be a pastor are watchful of what they say around me. They try to talk faith to me. But I hear things, and some of it grieves me. I hear people laughing and saying, "If I did not have to be here and Pastor wasn't around, I would be doing this and that." That kind of stuff is not funny to me. They are basically coming to church for show. They are not walking out the high calling in Christ Jesus. People, pastors included, do not save us, make us, or break us. We write our own destiny. We must learn to watch what we say because there is great power in our mouths. In addition, Jesus Himself said that our words are an accurate indication of the condition of our hearts. Listening to people, it does not take very long to find out where they are spiritually.

The Bible also says that our words are a spiritual force that should be used as an instrument to bring deliverance to those who are in captivity. Are our mouths being used in that capacity? With our mouths, we should be setting people free from oppression, not putting them in bondage. In God's sight, when we gossip, we are issuing forth profanities when we should be operating in His honor. Too many of us "roast" our pastor after church during lunch. Then, there are those who are super holy, who call others and spread gossip under the guise of prayer. You can imagine them thinking, *We're only telling them so they can pray, aren't we?*

Too often we are deceived. We are gossiping even though we do not call it that. No, we use nicer words than that, like *sharing*, and *helping*. In truth, God has never asked anybody to call everybody in town and tell them everything that is going on so they can pray. Oh sure, He wants you to pray, but remember that love covers a multitude of sins.

The Bible says that Jesus cast out demons by the words of His mouth. We either flow in the power of God or we flow in the powers of the flesh. One or the other is guiding our lives. When we come into the presence of God, our lips should continue to release His awesome presence and give Him liberty to minister among the people. But, too often we come to Him with defiled lips, and our praise does not go very high.

How do we defile our lips? We do that in obvious ways, such as when cursing and allowing profanities to escape from our mouths, but we also do it in ways that are less obvious. When we engage in ungodly conversations, gossip and cause strife, or backbite and belittle people, our mouths can no longer be considered an instrument of life. This is a serious issue, my brothers and sisters. With our mouths we have destroyed people, and then we come to church and sing praises to God.

Who are you and I fooling? We might have deceived ourselves that everything is fine, but we certainly have not fooled God. He heard every word of it, and can read our minds, too. Some saints have bumper stickers on their cars that say, "Honk if you love Jesus," and when somebody honks, the poor, unsuspecting soul gets a piece of mind they did not expect. The other driver was just responding to the bumper sticker, while the owner just happened to forget he had the sticker on his bumper. You can imagine what the bumper sticker owner must think, *Get out of my way! Can't you see I'm on the way to church to worship God?* It would be funny if it were not so true.

My friends, we are either going to flow in the power of God or we are going to move in the power of the flesh—one or the other. We are the ones who choose our pathway every hour of every day.

It is vital that our lips remain clean. Perhaps it would be a good idea for all of us to go back to the law and review the ordinances of cleansing that had to take place before one could participate in the sacrifices and the offerings dealing with the shedding of sacrificial blood. There was an enormous amount of cleansing that took place continually or they could not proceed further:

> In the year that king Uzziah died I saw also the Lord sitting upon a throne, high and lifted up, and his train filled the temple. Above it stood the seraphims: each one had six wings; with twain he covered his face, and with twain he covered his feet, and with twain he did fly. And one cried unto another, and said, Holy, holy, holy, is the Lord of hosts: the whole earth is full of his glory. And the posts of the door moved at the voice of him that cried, and the house was filled with smoke. Then said I, Woe is me! for I am undone; because I am a man of unclean lips, and I dwell in the midst of a people of unclean lips: for mine eyes have seen the King, the Lord of hosts.
>
> —Isaiah 6:1–5

Isaiah was a pretty good fellow, don't you think? He was a wonderful, true prophet of the Lord, but he said, "Woe is me." We know what happened. A seraphim came to him with a live coal off of the altar and laid it on Isaiah's mouth. In this act, his iniquity was taken away, and his sin was purged. I want you to clearly see the importance of clean lips and a clean mouth.

What about our hands? Our hands are instruments of healing through which God can work; and they are tools to defeat the powers of darkness. Glory to God that we have such a tool! Do you remember the ninth plague that occurred to the Egyptians under Moses' command?

> And the LORD said unto Moses, Stretch out thine hand toward heaven, that there may be darkness over the land of Egypt, even darkness which may be felt. And Moses stretched forth his hand toward heaven; and there was a thick darkness in all the land of Egypt three days: They saw not one another, neither rose any from his place for three days: but all the children of Israel had light in their dwellings.
>
> —EXODUS 10:21–23

Moses never said a word. He just stretched his hand toward heaven and the darkness came. Do you remember the battle that the children of Israel faced with Amalek?

> Then came Amalek, and fought with Israel in Rephidim. And Moses said unto Joshua, Choose us out men, and go out, fight with Amalek: to morrow I will stand on the top of the hill with the rod of God in mine hand. So Joshua did as Moses had said to him, and fought with Amalek: and Moses, Aaron, and Hur went up to the top of the hill. And it came to pass, when Moses

held up his hand, that Israel prevailed: and when he let down his hand, Amalek prevailed. But Moses' hands were heavy; and they took a stone, and put it under him, and he sat thereon; and Aaron and Hur stayed up his hands, the one on the one side, and the other on the other side; and his hands were steady until the going down of the sun.

—EXODUS 17:8–12

There were no words involved here either, just the hands. I am saying our hands are important in the work of God, and they must not be allowed to be defiled. Let's look at a Scripture passage in the Book of Habakkuk:

O LORD, I have heard thy speech, and was afraid: O LORD, revive thy work in the midst of the years, in the midst of the years make known; in wrath remember mercy. God came from Teman, and the Holy One from mount Paran. Selah. His glory covered the heavens, and the earth was full of his praise. And his brightness was as the light; he had horns coming out of his hand: and there was the hiding of his power.

—HABAKKUK 3:2–4

There is something very interesting here that you need to see. I looked up that verse and the words that were translated "horns coming out of his hand," and here is what I found. According to *Strong's Exhaustive Concordance*, the horns refer to rays of light. So, out of God's fingertips—hear this now—come streams of light that split the atmosphere. Out of His hands flow these rays of light and in His hands is His power. Listen up! This is going to propel us forward.

You and I are made in the likeness and the image of

God, aren't we? We are commanded to lift up holy hands unto God and to lay hands on the sick. It was not just a suggestion or an option from God; we are supposed to do it. If God's power is in His hand, as it says in this passage, and we are made in His image, then the power of God is released through our hands in a stream of light as well. Praise God and hallelujah! If our hands are defiled, we may still have a little of God's power in our hands, but it is like turning on a flashlight that has mud caked over the lens. Regrettably, God is unable to work through us and release His power when our hands are defiled.

How do we defile our hands? Well, everything from sexual sin to corrupt business practices and everything in between. When we cheat on our income taxes or participate in under-the-table dirty deals, we become dirty. When we habitually reach out and participate in things of the world and grab hold of things in this world's system, our hands get defiled.

Let me take it a step further. Spiritually defiled, unclean people surround us all the time. That is exactly why we are to use the blood of Jesus daily to cleanse ourselves. Use the blood like natural soap. In the medical profession, doctors wash their hands when they move from one patient to the next, and we should do the same in the spirit realm.

Allow me to reveal my heart: there have been occasions when I ministered in healing lines and have laid hands on certain people and literally felt the defilement attached to them. Everyone who comes to be prayed for is not necessarily coming for the right reasons. The power of God would stop and I never understood why. In the past, I did not know what to do, but I do now (claim the blood of Jesus and receive my cleansing). Glory to God forevermore.

God always has an answer to every dilemma we bump into. Hallelujah!

> Who shall ascend into the hill of the LORD? or who shall stand in his holy place? He that hath clean hands, and a pure heart; who hath not lifted up his soul unto vanity, nor sworn deceitfully.
>
> —PSALM 24:3–4

We simply cannot get into the presence of God if we do not have clean hands. Once we are cleansed—our mouths, hands, and hearts washed clean by the blood of the Lamb—we can come into His presence and worship our magnificent God. Our hands are raised in adoration to Him. Think of what is happening in the spirit dimension. Hundreds, perhaps even thousands, of hands are raised toward heaven, and out of every finger, light radiates and pierces the darkness, sending out beacons of light. Can we even imagine such a glorious thing? Yet, according to God's holy Word, that is exactly what happens when we come to Him pure.

If all of us were to come before Him like that, can you imagine what could happen? Your church would be absolutely filled with the light of God. If multiplied thousands of churches all over this nation would grasp and act on this revelation, then the gospel light would penetrate every dark region of this country and the world. Evangelism would explode. I am telling you, church, this is real.

One time after I taught this, people went back to their workplace to put it to work. These people did not say anything to anyone, but waved their arms in trouble spots, believing God to bring light into the dark areas of their employment locales. In every single incident, in every single location this was done, the atmosphere immediately changed in their favor. We just do not know what power we have been given in our hands, do we?

Let me tell you a true story that happened to me years ago. At the close of a service one Sunday morning, I stepped down from the platform while the congregation stood to be dismissed. It was a particularly large group that day; it was a packed house. In stature, I am relatively short, and I could not see the people in the back of the room. I pointed my finger and waved my hand to indicate the location of someone to whom God wanted to minister. All of the sudden, *Wham! Bam! Bam!* Folding chairs on which the worshipers were seated flew in every direction. I did not see what caused it, and I did not know what happened. I just heard the commotion. I waited a moment to see if we could find out what happened, but I went ahead and dismissed the crowd when no one spoke up.

Moments after the service was over, a very large man strutted to the front of the room where I was standing and asked me pointedly, "Where did you get that power in your hands?" When I asked him what he was talking about, he continued, "When you did like that, moved your hand and pointed your finger in my direction, out of your finger came a bolt of light that went through the congregation, hit me in the head, and knocked me out." I did not know it at the time, but, glory to God, the man was a warlock and wanted to know where I got that kind of power because he wanted it. "His name is Jesus," I exclaimed. Raise those hands, my brothers and sisters, and let's cause havoc in the kingdom of darkness! Thank You, Jesus.

Interestingly, that man is not the only person who has asked me such a question. We need to be cognizant of what our actions can accomplish in the spirit realm. I have been in church services and snapped my fingers and had people fall out as if they had been knocked down with a two-by-four. In one meeting, I raised my hands and pointed towards the congregation, and about four hundred people hit the floor at the same time. I did not see it, but all of them claimed they saw fire shoot out of my hands. Praise His name. He is absolutely wonderful.

> When men are cast down, then thou shalt say, There is lifting up; and he shall save the humble person. He shall deliver the island of the innocent: and it is delivered by the pureness of thine hands.
>
> —Job 22:29–30

> And when ye spread forth your hands, I will hide mine eyes from you: yea, when ye make many prayers, I will not hear: your hands are full of blood.
>
> —Isaiah 1:15

There is delivering power in our hands, but if they are defiled, or our hearts are not pure, our prayers are not heard. Another area of concern is our ears. It is a sad thing when we cannot hear from God. The Bible constantly says, "Let him that has ears, hear" (Rev. 2:7). Everyone has some little something on the side of their head, some bigger than others. Some of us have little dainty ears and some of us have big ears. But that is not the ear He is talking about. As a matter of fact, we can be deaf as a doornail in the natural and still be spiritually tuned in to the things of God. It's sad when we cannot hear or see into that spirit realm, because we will flounder. There is a children's song that has great wisdom in its words: "Be careful little ears what you hear, be careful little eyes what you see."

I have preached this over and over again, and some have gotten bold enough to do it, although most people have not. Do not let others use your ears as garbage pails. Do not let them call and gossip and speak against leadership of the church or against your friends. Just say, "I am sorry, but my ears are not garbage pails. Good-bye, I'll see you in church."

We need to protect our faith and our spirit. If the television broadcasts bring all kinds of junk into our home, filled with all kinds of perversion and sin, then my question is, Why do we even allow it in our homes and watch it? Some might inevitably answer, "Well, it just came with the cable package." That package has now allowed all manner of hideous, horrid, disgusting filth to cascade into our houses like a tsunami of evil, festering, repugnant sin. Sorry to say we are actually paying to have that mess brought into our homes. Have we forgotten about the Spirit realm, and that there are things called evil spirits just waiting for the tiniest crack in the door into our lives? We need to wake up and be wise concerning both the natural and spiritual arenas.

Let's move on. Sometimes we happen into things out of ignorance, but don't get stuck there. The best is yet to come—our privileges as a priest.

seven

Me? A Priest?

Therefore if any man be in Christ, he is a new creature: old things are passed away; behold, all things are become new. And all things are of God, who hath reconciled us to himself by Jesus Christ, and hath given to us the ministry of reconciliation.

—2 Corinthians 5:17–18

Glory to God! All things become new at the moment of our new birth in the Spirit realm. That is tough to grasp. I remember when I first heard that. I used to look at my life and think, "It doesn't seem new to me." I did not act new. As a matter of fact, not one thing appeared new to me, but actually looked worse, because I did not have an understanding of spiritual things. It is our spirit man that is new. It is our spirit man that responds to God. Praise Him! Our spirit, the *real man*, is no longer required to obey the devil. We have a new Master, a new King, who is good and full of mercy.

Look at 2 Corinthians 5:18 again. God said we are ministers, every one of us. We are to minister this reconciliation to the world that does not yet know Him. We are to tell them, "God is not mad with you. He loves you. He wants to bless you and wants you in His household. He wants to dwell within you, so He can be that Friend that sticks closer to you than a brother." That is good news. We are appointed, anointed, and chosen by God Himself to be ministers of reconciliation. That is who we are. Every one of us has that ministry. Every one of us is a minister in the eyes of God, not just those behind the pulpit. We are all priests in His eyes. Let's look at a few more scriptures that establish that truth:

> Wherefore laying aside all malice, and all guile, and hypocrisies, and envies, and all evil speakings, As newborn babes, desire the sincere milk of the word, that ye may grow thereby: If so be ye have tasted that the Lord is gracious. To whom coming, as unto a living stone, disallowed indeed of men, but chosen of God, and precious, Ye also, as lively stones, are built up a spiritual house, an holy priesthood, to offer up spiritual sacrifices, acceptable to God by Jesus Christ.
>
> —1 PETER 2:1–5

We are a holy priesthood. When Jesus came, He not only fulfilled that, but He fulfilled that for us. He put in order a new covenant that is a better spiritual covenant. In verse 5, notice what the priesthood is supposed to do. We are to offer up spiritual sacrifices. We can apply the blood of Jesus to our heart so that our hard heart of unbelief can become soft before Him. What is equally as wonderful is that we, as priests before God, can apply the blood to our brothers and sisters in the Lord to release Him to delve into their heart to help them.

We can even act as a priest and apply the blood to those who do not know Him. God purposely built us up to be a spiritual house, a holy priesthood to offer up spiritual sacrifices acceptable to Him by Jesus Christ to reconcile men unto God.

> But ye are a chosen generation, a royal priesthood, an holy nation, a peculiar people; that ye should shew forth the praises of him who hath called you out of darkness into his marvellous light.
>
> —1 PETER 2:9

We know about being peculiar, don't we? We are quite familiar with that part, but why is it that we know more about that than being a royal priesthood. We go around saying, "We are peculiar," and some of us extend beyond the boundaries of peculiar. But the priesthood is the more important part of our character.

> And hath made us kings and priests unto God and his Father; to him be glory and dominion for ever and ever. Amen.
>
> —REVELATION 1:6

> And hast made us unto our God kings and priests: and we shall reign on the earth.
>
> —REVELATION 5:10

> Blessed and holy is he that hath part in the first resurrection: on such the second death hath no power, but they shall be priests of God and of Christ, and shall reign with him a thousand years.
>
> —REVELATION 20:6

Well, we are kings and we are priests—it is very clear. The King rules and reigns, and although we stand in that role when we take authority, that part of us will show forth more in the millenium and eternity when we rule and reign with King Jesus. We like having dominion. But, we have been pretty weak on our priestly role, which is where our hearts need to be centered now. We need to be excited that we have some authority as a priest to change people's hard hearts for God. In fact, the priestly part of our responsibilities is what moves us into the kingship part.

Being a priest does not mean we are talking about wearing a suit with our collar turned around. I know the root of that tradition, but realize that the collar is merely a symbol that some spiritual leaders use to set themselves apart. It is perfectly fine to do that, but it does not have any spiritual connotation to it. If you want to wear a collar, wear one.

I have spent many hours researching the functions of a priest. In the Bible, the functions do not change over time. What the biblical priests did in the natural, we do now in the spirit. You are going to love this. The chief function is the care of the vessels of the sanctuary and the sacrificial duties of the altar. We can be vessels of honor or vessels of dishonor. (See 2 Tim. 2:20.) It certainly would not take much time to discover that here people are the vessels that God is referring to.

Only the priests may offer sacrifices of any kind. (See Num. 18:5, 7.) The priests also give instruction in the ways and requirements of God. I am not talking about the High Priest. I am talking about priests. They are the authority regarding the law and an agent of revelation to the people. Now this is great. The priests are the custodians of the medical arena and play an important part safeguarding the health of the community. (See Lev. 13:15.) Did you get that? People wonder if we are to lay hands on the sick to be healed. According to the law, the priests are to be custodians of the medical arena, and a safeguard to the health of the community.

According to these scriptures, we are priests unto God *now*; not just when we get to heaven, and not only if and when we ever get behind a pulpit. We are declared to be priests from the moment of our new birth to apply the blood of Jesus. For what reason? Reconciliation of every kind. God wants us to live our lives as priests before Him, applying the blood to bring people back in fellowship with God and soundness to their lives. Thank You, Jesus. That is something to be happy about, my friends.

The Word of God calls us priests. Out of the mouths of two or three witnesses, let a thing be established. (See Deut. 19:15). Priests are administrators of justice, to see that those who have been defiled are reconsecrated to the Lord. They ensure that those who have been defiled, those who are dirty, common, stained, or wounded, are reconciled back to God. The world is waiting for us to take our place. Surely, there is no hope for them without us being what God has ordained us to be. They also blow the trumpets that summon the people to war or for the keeping of a feast. Priests may also bless in the name of the Lord. Are you listening to me? Are you grasping the privilege we have been given? We are talking about who the Bible says we are.

We are born into God's kingdom a priest, not made to become one. We must learn how to operate in this office. In the Spirit realm, we are defiled when we are around people who are spiritually dead. But as a priest, we can be cleansed from this defilement by the blood. Also, we can apply the blood to that person's hard heart so they can be reconciled to God.

A ministry of reconciliation is the ministry of a priest. That is what they do; they mediate between man and God. We all need people serving in their spiritual capacity as our priest. We all need godly council and explanation of the Word of God. We all need correction and admonition to stay on the right path. Thank God for those in the body of Christ who have been operating in that capacity. No doubt, they have been overwhelmed with the needs of people. All of us should have been walking in our priestly responsibilities and privileges, but it was left on the shoulders of a few.

Priests were the ones who took the blood to the altar and applied it there as a holy sacrifice. We need to take advantage of the shed blood of Jesus for our families and their deliverance. Do you know what has held people captive? My Bible tells me, in 2 Corinthians 4:4, that deception and blindness are the culprits, but the blood of Jesus is well able to wash that mess away and open their eyes. You can pray for Joe Blow down the street, who has been driving you bananas, covering him in the blood of Jesus, and then watch him change and move into the things of God. All you are doing is operating in your office as a priest, ordained of God to do so.

Yes, Jesus fulfilled the law. He is still the morning and evening Sacrifice; and He did it just for us. He fulfilled the law so that He could make it applicable to our lives. But we have to apply this truth. We have to get involved in what Jesus has accomplished for us.

Priests had to have pure hearts. Some of us have crusty

old hearts, and we have to cleanse them to penetrate them with the blood to get results. The more we apply it in faith, the softer the heart gets. Is our heart pure, or do we have heart problems? Let's take a look at the five characteristics of heart trouble and see where we measure up:

1. When people have heart trouble, they have no power over sin. In other words, these people are constantly doing the same thing over and over and over again. They do not necessarily want to do anything about it in the first place. We can talk to them until we are blue in the face, and it is just like talking to a tree. There are multitudes who cannot seem to help themselves. They want to, but they cannot. They try, but they just do not ever make it. They are on the edge, but never seem to make it in, flip-flopping from the church to the darkness of worldly things. There are many in church who get trapped in the biggest cycles I have ever seen in my life; just round and round the mulberry bush, because they are not willing to deal with their sinful behavior.

   We can have a perfect heart one day and lose it by nightfall because we get defiled. If we do not stay in the Word of God for daily instruction and keep ourselves cleansed by the blood of the Lamb, we can go down a wrong road to former habits without much thought. We need to act like King David did after his sin with Bathsheba. He said, "Lord, create in me a clean heart" (Ps. 51:10). The response of a person who has a perfect heart is that we are saddened by our sin. We are burdened by our sin and want to be free of it. If this is you, begin to say, "Hallelujah. I am going free of this thing—today. I have a heart problem and I need help." Thank God, we can get it.

2. Another symptom of heart trouble is whether we have a hunger for God and His Word and whether we have a willingness to be a doers of that Word. Do we like to apply the Word of God to our personal lives, or do we just like to hear it on occasion? Most of these people do not come to church, but that is not necessarily true all the time. We can be sitting in church and still have heart trouble. Do we really love the Word of God? Is it really life to us? If we have spiritual heart disease, it is difficult to love God's Word.

Let me say this, too—we cannot say we love God's Word and choose to stay away from church. That may be hard to swallow, but that is the truth. The Bible says that God's Word is medicine for whatever ails us. The Word about the blood of the Lamb can cleanse us and heal us from our heart trouble. God is indeed our Helper and Deliverer.

3. Those of us who have heart problems most often have attitudes of unbelief and carnality. Basically, unbelief is just another form of carnality. The Bible is clear, the carnal mind does not receive anything from God. He is spirit and we must hear and receive from Him with the spirit. People come to a church service and receive nothing from it. We question everything, wondering whether it was a movement of God or not? We think in the carnal realm because we cannot keep tuned in to the

things of God. Everything that takes place in the service is rationalized back to the natural realm while we fail to understand spiritual things.

We are spirit, but most of us often let our flesh rule us, don't we? God's intent is that the spirit man, the part of us that is born again and is made in the image of God, rules the flesh from within which it dwells.

4. People with heart problems are not givers. When I hear someone say something like, "I knew she'd get around to money. See there, preachers cannot say anything without talking about money," I know that that is a carnal mind talking. God loves a cheerful giver, but these people are neither givers nor tithers. As a matter of fact, they nickel and dime God. Let's examine ourselves. Are we greedy, tending to hold on to our money, refusing to turn it loose when prompted by the Lord? Are we looking for opportunities to give or do we cringe when offering time comes around?

5. A final symptom of someone with spiritual heart disease is a lack of hunger for the things and the presence of God. Because that is not where their hearts are, they are unaware of His presence. They have no earthly idea of whether He is in the room or not; they are not spirit-centered. Have you ever been in a time of praise and worship and the song leader kept singing the same song over and over again? The anointing gets on a song and if they are sensitive to the move of God's Spirit, they will stay with that song because the anointing can destroy the yokes of bondage. If the worship leader moves

to a new song too soon, the anointing will lift, and it will be very obvious to those who are in the spirit. People with spiritual heart trouble have great difficulty flowing with God because they are unable to recognize His presence when He walks in. This may come as a shocker, but He does not show up in every church service in supernatural ways because He can't bless every church service. It has a lot to do with the hearts and the attitudes of the people and whether or not there is sin in the camp.

Yes, pastors need to preach against sin, but if we are even in the least measure sensitive to God, we know when we are in sin. When we are first saved we may not know exactly what we have done, but we will know something is wrong because something will have changed on the inside of us. We have all experienced that and the more we know about His Word, the more precisely we can pinpoint our error.

Heart problems are tough to deal with in people. If we could have changed people's hearts, we would have done it many years ago. We have tried every strategy. Am I right? We have tried the nice approach, and we have tried the mean approach. We have screamed at them, yelled at them, and begged them to come back to God. We have talked to them about hell, wrote note after note to them—"We love you; we miss you; we want you to come back"—but they just look at us. It takes the Spirit of God to deal with the hearts of men.

If left untended for any period of time, our heart will grow hard. Scripture says, "As a man thinketh in his heart, so is he" (Prov. 23:7). If our heart reveals to others what kind of people we actually are, then it is apparent we are going to have to deal with people (ourselves included) at the heart level. That, my friend, will take the power of God and the precious blood of Jesus.

Basically, heart problems set in because we have not renewed our minds with the Word of God and cleansed ourselves daily with the blood. In truth, we can have a clean heart this morning and not have one tonight. Sometimes, we can be defiled by the world and our heart be turned away from God and down a dead-end road. We desperately need the blood of the Lamb applied to our hearts as the morning and evening sacrifice.

We are talking about the things of the heart. Maybe you know people who do not respond to the things of the Lord. There is a real good chance they have heart problems. Maybe it is you. Perhaps you have difficulties. You have prayed, others pray for you and lay hands on you, yet nothing changes. Have the things of the Lord grown dim to you? Have you lost the intense interest you had in His church and His Word? Has the excitement and fire waned from your bones? We normally think that everyone else has changed, then we tend to throw the blame on them. It is time just to get honest. We ought to admit to ourselves and the Lord Jesus that we have heart problems. Look at yourself right now. It is really important to do this self-examination, saints, because you do not want to become hardened to sin. If we do, believe it or not, we will become indifferent to sin and will not want to repent—and this is not a good thing.

You may be thinking, *I don't feel like a priest.* This position is not based on feelings. We are simply stating something that God has already declared over us. Welcome to the light, my friend. Come out of the darkness and into the light because *you are a priest unto God.* The devil does not want us to see this because some of us are going to believe it. Some of us will have the audacity to start acting like a priest. The devil will shake to his core because he is fully aware that things will start happening in the hearts of men. It will not be a pretty picture for him.

The only thing Satan can do is hit us a few times, try to knock us down, wear us down to quit fighting, or try to bring depression on us. Listen, that is why we were given the full armor of God. It will quench every fiery dart of the enemy. One thing we need to remember is this—never give up! God has already made us more than conquerors.

It is not surprising, though, that when we begin acting like a priest, the people we are praying for begin acting up, usually worse than they were. The devil is trying to hang on to his control over people. He has them lash out, but a lot of times the arrow comes straight at us. The blood of Jesus will bring captives out of the darkness and into the light, but let me give you a word of caution that might save you some anguish. When you begin to walk in your role as a priest, do not go up to that person and say, "Stupid, I am applying the blood of Jesus to you in hopes of turning you around." It is better to do this in our prayer time alone with God, and let Him work unhindered. Too many times people will fight us, and yes, they will do things they know aggravate us even though they know we are praying for them. We should not have to say these sorts of things, but sometimes it is still necessary. Let's pray and let God work.

We need to come in as a minister of reconciliation and let people know that Jesus loves them and cares greatly about them and about what's going on in their lives. Yes, some of them will look at us funny, but some will respond, "Man, I needed to hear that!" People need to hear good news. They need to hear that their situation is not hopeless.

The priest is the one ordained to give out that good news. It is fabulous to work hand in glove with almighty God. What a privilege we have been given! What joy to see the lives of people turn around into victory! We are a blessed people. We can do this.

eight

Bridging the Gap

SAY THIS OUT LOUD, "YES, I am a priest before almighty God, and my ministry is reconciliation!" Doesn't that sound fabulous? Whoever we are, whatever we are doing, wherever we might be, we are commissioned to reconcile back to God those people who are not walking with Him. What an honor! Above all, we ought to be ever aware that we are ministers. If we see somebody that has a sad and lonely face with no apparent hope for life in them, we are to walk as the light of the world and introduce them to the One who can turn their lives around.

Some of you big men think that you are only supposed to be out making a living. You are a minister of reconciliation and you can go in places that we ladies cannot easily go. It takes a man to talk to a man most of the time. God needs the involvement of His men. You might think that you are in that job you have because you are an expert in that field of study, but you are really there because God put you there. You did not get that job on your own. The steps of a righteous man are ordered of the Lord—isn't that what Scripture says? (See Ps. 37:23.) He has already established the things that He wants us to accomplish. Hell cannot stop what God is doing in our lives if we are determined to flow with God. We are not a ship lost at sea, bouncing around here and there. We are on a divine mission in life, and it is not mission impossible. With man, it might be impossible, but not so when God is involved. Let me remind you, we are not doing these things with the arm of man, but by the power of God.

We should be coming toward people with our spiritual antennas up, expecting to hear God's voice. He will tell us what each person needs to hear and how to minister to each individual. We should be planting heavenly "seeds" straight from the throne of God, knowing that He will send others to water them. We need to wake up, church, and understand that time is so short, and we have to get our act together. But we need to be sound and whole to fulfill our potential. Do not get caught up in religion and say, "They have been looking for Jesus a long time," because we are much closer than we were. The sheer fact we have been looking so long ought to motivate us to get with the program. We are the only ministers of reconciliation God has to work through. The amazing thing is that He thinks we are sufficient. He believes we can do the job—and we can.

You might be working in a hard place. Do you know what that says to me? God knows what He put in you, and knows you have the nature to handle it. He knows that you and you alone can go into that place and do His work completely, effectively, and successfully. Wow! Here we are, complaining all the way. Almighty God put you there because there is something special about your nature, your character, something about your attributes that you can do it when others cannot and drop out. He brought you—on purpose—into that darkness as a light, as a minister of reconciliation, because you have what it takes to plow in there and pull down the forces that have held the people in captivity. You are in contact with the pit to pull them out. God does not want to lose even one person.

We may think we would like to work with a bunch of Christians, but let me tell you, if they are not walking submissively to God under the cleansing power of the blood of Jesus, it can be very disappointing. Christians who do not walk under the blood of the Lamb get religious, and their hearts harden so that it becomes unteachable. There is nothing like dealing with a religious spirit. They will tell you they are washed in the blood and have received their prayer language—but some of them can be backbiters.

What a God we have! Take advantage of the blood of Jesus for your families. You men of the church, learn the value of pleading the blood over your household. Men—you are the priests of your house as well as priests unto God. Women—if you are single, or if your husband does not assume his priestly role, do not get discouraged. You can still apply the blood to your homes and families and get the same results and have the same benefits; after all, you are a priest according to the Word of God. What a difference can be made when you actually do this. Children can be set free and come back to God. In these years that are in front of us, you are going to need to know what I am teaching you now, because we are quickly moving into very perilous times. Your families are depending upon you.

People who are caught in sin are blinded to truth, and we have been ordained of God to take the blood of Jesus and clear out that blindness to shed the scales from their eyes. Somebody has to do it—who else will do it besides God's people?

What is reconciliation? We have talked around it but listen to this wonderful definition: the process by which God and man are brought together again. The Bible teaches that God and man are alienated from each other because of God's holiness and man's sinfulness. That is it in a nutshell. God is there. We are here. Somebody had to bridge the gap. We could not go to Him, so He came to us through our Lord Jesus Christ. Jesus came down to our level—tempted of every sin, well-acquainted with our infirmities and weaknesses—for the sole purpose of raising us up to live with Him. Praise God forevermore!

Some of us get to thinking, *Poor, pitiful me*, when in truth God came after us. He knows us so well, and yet loved us enough to send the love of His heart as our personal Sacrifice. He chose you and He chose me, and thought we were well worth the cost. This is too fabulous to believe! Even if we have made a mess of our lives, we are still chosen of God. That is what reconciliation is all about.

You know, I do not fully understand how reconciliation works or how He does it. But, I sure am glad He does it. In the natural, I do not understand how the lights in my house work. I just throw a switch and they are supposed to come on. I do not know how my car works. I put in gas, I turn a key, and off I go, right? We do not have to identify every wire or comprehend every gizmo under the hood. We leave that to the mechanics or the electricians. We just trust that whoever developed that thing knew what they were doing.

Why can't we trust God that way? Why can't we, at face value, trust that whoever wrote the Bible knew what He was doing? His name is the Holy Spirit, and—hallelujah—the Author of this book lives inside each of us. Let's just trust Him, shall we? Why do we stumble with that? Let's just believe what He said and get on with the program of being what God says we can be. This whole concept of reconciliation can be life transforming if we can grab it.

Although God loves the sinner, it is impossible for Him not to judge the sin that man has committed. God took the initiative in reconciliation. We did not work this plan out. Simply put, He wanted us and came to get us. Scripture says that while we were still sinners and enemies, Christ died for us. (See Rom. 5:6–10.) That is amazing to me. Jesus said, "Yes, I see the mess your life is in, but I've come to get you while in the mess so that I can get you out of the mess" (Rom. 5:6–10).

We cannot clean ourselves up, but, oh, how hard we have tried. It takes the Spirit of God to do that. The plan of reconciliation is already in place on our behalf. All believers are ministers. That is a separate group from the five-fold ministry, those who have been licensed and ordained. When someone asks, "Will all of the ministers stand up?" every believer should stand to their feet. Praise God. Until we recognize who we really are, we will be ineffective in the kingdom of God. We have had this thing all messed up—it is Jesus and Jesus alone. It has nothing to do with us. It was His plan from the beginning.

There are so many Christians who desperately need to be set free. A lot of times, we are in bondage and do not know it, funny as it may seem. It is evident, though. We are at church, but we are not doing the things we should be doing for the kingdom of God. We have too many benchwarmers, too many people who never do a thing to help anybody. They come in on Sunday morning and leave. I believe they think church has nothing to do with life. It is just a ritual; something they do on Sunday.

It is not only our privilege, but it is our responsibility to walk the steps of a minister of reconciliation. Amazing as it sounds, God needs us. He has chosen to work His plan through us. This is part of the reason why we are left on Earth after we are born again. We are the hands of Jesus, the mouth of Jesus, and the feet of Jesus. The blood of the Lamb has brought us into this ministry, and this is the reason that we can be effective in the calling He has placed on our lives.

The church frequently appears not to care that the world is going to hell. We have become a self-centered, pious "country club," with all its social and dining activities. That grieves the heart of our Father. He never has stayed behind the stained glass windows. He likes to be out on the highways and byways giving people an opportunity to come into His house.

So many people are absolutely hopeless because the world has nothing to offer. But, we can tell people the good news: "Your life can be different. Jesus knows you and truly does care for you." What a great message of life He has for a dying world. I am telling you the truth, the world is starved to hear that message. In fact, those of us who are born again do not have a right to stay silent about Jesus Christ and what He has done for us. I believe we will give an account for keeping salvation to ourselves and holding it when it was given to us freely to share. We cannot keep quiet about our salvation when our neighbor is going to split the gates of hell wide open. I believe there will be a day of reckoning. There is a judgment seat, and we will give an answer for what we have done or not done with this so great a salvation. We may not know how to do anything, but we have a mouth, feet, and hands. We can give our testimony.

If you find yourself in this place today, you know that you are not walking as a minister of reconciliation. In fact, you may not even like people. You just want them to leave you alone. The blood needs to be applied to your heart. We were not saved just to sit in church on Sunday and disregard the needs of the people or the situations they are facing Monday through Saturday. The entire point of this ministry is love, love, love. How can we know that we are saved? We love.

Many in the church are sick in their bodies and minds simply because they are not walking in love with other people. Oh, they claim to know how to do everything, but in their hearts, they are not walking in love. We have to get this thing, brothers and sisters. This is our calling.

Father, in the name of Jesus, I ask You to deal with the heart of every person reading this book. As a priest before You, I apply the precious blood of Jesus to the deep places of our hearts. May the blood massage and strip away the hardness, blindness, and lies that have kept us from walking the high life by Your side. May You give each of us a boldness to be vocal about Your goodness toward mankind. May the blood deal with every heart problem that has hindered us and kept us captive and ineffective from completing Your plans and purposes. Enable us to walk as the light of Your gospel in the midst of this dark world, and give us a deeper compassion to reach out for those still chained to that darkness. May the blood of Jesus saturate us, that we may have ears to hear, eyes to see, mouths to be used for

Your glory, feet ready to go where Your Spirit leads us, and hands to be extended to bring deliverance to the captives. We thank You. You are our morning and evening Sacrifice, and we welcome Your work in our hearts. We know the blood of Jesus is changing us. We give You glory and praise in Jesus' name. Amen.

nine

Sin Versus Iniquity

This is the covenant that I will make with them after those days, saith the Lord, I will put my laws into their hearts, and in their minds will I write them; And their sins and iniquities will I remember no more.

—HEBREWS 10:16–17

HOW IS HE GOING TO put the law, the Word, into our hearts? Remember, we are talking about the heart as the center of our soulish area. As we renew our mind with the Word of God, then our soul is saved by the engrafted Word, and God will write the Word *on* our hearts. When we finally get our mind and spirit working together, we are a powerful force for God's agenda.

When the miraculous new birth takes place in each of us, God's methods and instructions do not instantly appear in our heart. It certainly would be wonderful to immediately know the ways of God, but we do not. We have all found that out, I am sure. "No," He said, "I will put my laws into their hearts, and in their minds will I write them" (Jer. 31:33). That says to me that if we will abide under the power of the blood of Jesus, if we will let the blood do its work in our heart, then God says, "On your cleansed heart I will imprint my laws so that My Words can become a part of you and regulate you from the inside…and in your mind I will surely write them. I will write My precepts; I will write My Covenant; I will write My will [His Word is His will…] and My ways in your mind" (Jer. 31:33). Glory to God! Can you imagine such a thing? Isn't that absolutely wonderful? That no matter what situation we find ourselves in, bless God, we'd automatically think the thoughts of God. No matter what happens to us, our hearts would instinctively respond toward someone according to the ways of God. Just that alone would save us from a multitude of problems and subsequent anguish.

Knowing that our cardinal law is love, is there anyone who would not want to have a loving heart toward everybody? I know in myself, that when I begin to feel something rise up within me against someone, I am disturbed that I feel that way because I hate it. I want to walk in love. I do not like harboring things in my heart because it really bothers me. I literally fight tooth and nail to block access of any detrimental feelings into my heart.

This is something that God Himself wants to do for all of us. This is not some far-fetched something, but His plan from the beginning. "This is the covenant that I will make with them after those days" (Heb. 10:16). He is talking about the days after we allow the blood to do its work in our hearts and lives. As we apply the blood, walk under the blood, believe the blood, and as we gain the knowledge of the reality of the blood and allow it to penetrate us, God makes our hearts soft and pliable and responsive to Him so we can think from a heavenly perspective. What a mighty God we serve, love, and hold dear! Thinking the thoughts of God—what a thrill. This is not beyond reach for any of us. This has been the plan of God for each one of us from the beginning.

That scripture really tells us that when we apply the blood, believe in the blood, and walk under the covering of the blood, then there is no remembrance of sins or iniquities. I do not want to remember my sin. It thrills me to know that almighty God has completely forgotten about them. To tell you the truth, I have no intention of reminding Him of them. There are, however, plenty of people who will remind us and God about our sins and shortcomings, I assure you. As a matter of fact, it is unwise to come into the holy of holies, into the presence of the Most High God, with a "garbage pail" mouth full of gossip and slander about His sons and daughters and dump it at His feet. We might be talking about Sally and Joe, but if they are born again and covered with the blood of Jesus, they belong to Him even if they are not acting like it.

We have all done that at one time or another. We tend to judge ourselves on our good intentions, but scrutinize others in detail by their actions. We often demand virtues in others that we do not practice ourselves. Let's use the same standard of measurement for others as we use on ourselves, shall we?

When we come to Him talking about others, something normally gets stirred up and He says, "Let's talk about you. Let's look at the log in your own eye and deal with that first" (Matt. 7:3–5). Ouch. I do not know about you, but I'd prefer to avoid that situation. I would much rather that He see me garbed in glorious robes, washed white by the blood, and radiating the Lord Jesus Christ.

Let me back up a minute. Look at that verse again. Since they are listed separately, are sins and iniquities different?

> This is the covenant that I will make with them after those days, saith the Lord, I will put my laws into their hearts, and in their minds will I write them; And their sins and iniquities will I remember no more.
>
> —HEBREWS 10:16–17

> Who hath believed our report? and to whom is the arm of the LORD revealed? For he shall grow up before Him as a tender plant, and as a root out of a dry ground: he hath no form nor comeliness; and when we shall see him, there is no beauty that we should desire him. He is despised and rejected of men; a man of sorrows, and acquainted with grief: and we hid as it were our faces from him; he was despised, and we esteemed him not. Surely he hath borne our griefs, and carried our sorrows: yet we did esteem him stricken, smitten of God, and afflicted, But he was wounded for our transgressions, he was bruised for our iniquities: the chastisement of our peace was upon him; and with his stripes we are healed.
>
> —ISAIAH 53:1–5

Let's go into this a little bit more so we can understand it. We know that the Scripture in Isaiah is speaking of the Lord Jesus. There is a distinct difference between sin or transgressions and iniquities, but most of the church is not aware of it. Without knowledge that Jesus took care of both of them, we are hindered from being who God really wants us to be.

The word *transgression* means sin. He was wounded for our sin, or that thing we do that is contrary to God's Word. He dealt with sin, but as wonderful as this is, that in itself would not be enough for us because we keep sinning. What is it that keeps us doing the same dumb thing over and over and over and over? That, my friend, is iniquity. Isaiah saw that Jesus not only paid the price to free us from sin, but also from what keeps us sinning. By the blood of the Lamb, we can cut that sin off at the root. Praise God. There is hope for our hearts. It can be made as white as snow by His exceptional grace of love shown in the sacrifice of Jesus.

We can know Jesus is bigger than our sin problem, but if we do not know we *can* go or *how* to go to the *root* and how to eradicate that sin nature, we go round and round the mulberry bush. We commit the act, and cry, and repent, and cry, and repent. We tell ourselves, "I am not going to do that again," but by morning we have already eaten those words and repented again.

Listen, all of us have the same problem—we sin. We all make mistakes. Our lives can certainly be a mess. We can even be born-again, spirit-filled messes when we have not understood the great work He accomplished for us on the cross and through the Resurrection over death. From time to time, we have all felt empty and void because we have been defiled by past sin. We have been forgiven all right, but have remained wounded, stained, dirty, and common. Self-help groups and do-it-yourself improvement books may address symptoms, but they do not solve our problems. The blood of the Lamb is stronger and more powerful than any problem we have, inside or out. The more we understand what privileges and authority have been given to us as priests before God, the more victory we will experience in life. It is called the morning and evening Sacrifice. Over time, that thing which has been our downfall will forever come crumbling at our feet in defeat. Can we grasp this? This is a key to victorious living, not only for ourselves but for others to whom we apply the blood.

Isaiah said then that Jesus was wounded for the sins in our lives and was bruised for our iniquity. He took bruises for our iniquity—our sin nature—so that we might be free entirely. See, it is one thing to have sins forgiven; it is quite another thing to have its root cut out and walk free of sin's control. Hallelujah. That thing that haunts us in the night hours and aborts in shame our praise to God can fall to its knees in submission under the power of the blood of the High Priest of our profession.

We cannot do this on our own, but we can do it by faith in God's Word. We cannot break the power of sin or iniquity, but the blood that speaks of better things than Abel's blood can shatter it. Praise God forevermore. Our faith in God and His graces of provision, including that of our priestly mantle, activates this truth. In life, Christians can have drug and alcohol problems among other things. Yes, we can. Do not be too quick to judge. Most are brokenhearted about it and would do anything to stop it, but they just do not know how to get out from under the bondage and walk away. Those things are just escape mechanisms from deep hurt. All of us need to learn how to operate in God's kingdom once we are born again. We desperately need compassionate teachers and pastors that teach the way to freedom. Do not criticize; too many are yet in chains. We were all in bondage at one time.

Perhaps we might have problems with our children or our marriage. What about temper and attitude? Some of us have gone around in circles for years and years and years and years. We have screamed and yelled, and cried, repented, and then did the same dumb thing again.

We have wanted God to do it for us, never realizing that He has *already* done it for us. Do we really understand that? The work has been complete for thousands of years, all wrapped up in the blood of the Lamb. By faith, we enter into the blessings of God; and we must labor to enter into the rest of those blessings. (See Heb. 4:1–11.) We experience God by faith to the measure we can broaden ourselves to believe His provisions. How critical it is to be a part of a Word church—a church that teaches the Word accurately. We cannot just hear about the new birth every week. I mean, that's great for the sinner, but the saints starve to gain dimensions of faith to cover the many areas of life. Certainly, the new birth is the most important area of salvation, but it is not the only area. God sent Jesus so that we could have victory in every area: health, protection, prosperity, family, and any sort of problem.

We should be climbing from glory to glory, ever more closely conformed and aligned to the Lord Jesus Christ. We should look like Him, act like Him, and pray like Him, constantly gaining all of the victories that we need for ourselves and others. We build line upon line, precept upon precept. (See 2 Cor. 3:10; Isa. 28:10.) But, His Word will only work in those who believe His Word will work; it doesn't automatically happen simply because we belong to Him. That would be great if it were that way, but it is not. We are getting back to free will, we can walk in God as much as we want to. Here again, we can—should—put on our priestly robes and apply the blood to the hearts of people. Who in their right mind doesn't want success in all that they do? No one.

Just because someone dies and splits hell's gates wide

open does not mean that Jesus did not want that person in heaven. He desires all to repent and come to the knowledge of the truth. (See 1 Tim. 2:3–4.) That person either did not know the provision of forgiveness or was deceived and rejected it. The blood of the Lamb can be applied to their eyes, mind, and heart daily. The blood will remove the root of their problem—if we stay with it. Do not do it just one time and say, "It did not work." *The Word works and it works every time. The blood works and it works every time.* That's what I see so often in the church. Have you ever prayed for somebody and it is like you were praying for a dead tree? Over a period of time we just give up and say, "Forget it, if they want to go to hell, let 'em go! My hands are clean." Not so, my friend. Do not turn loose of the power of God in your life or in anybody else's. We have all gotten that frustrated with people, although we do not like to admit it. It's not very spiritual is it? Realize that we are dealing with blinded minds, hardened hearts, and sometimes even evil spirits. People are never our problem. although they appear to be so. There is no situation that the blood cannot resolve, no wound the blood cannot heal, and no stain the blood cannot remove. Stay with it, and then get ready for the thrill of your life. Glory to God!

ten

Too Hard for God?

A HEART OF FLESH IS A heart that is soft; one that is pliable in God's hands. What a great promise! That is the will of our Father that our stony heart be crumbled and replaced with one that responds to His voice. That is so good. I just want to shout. I know shouting makes a lot of people nervous, but it doesn't bother me any. God delivered me out of the pit, not just some little hole in the ground. I was way below ground level when God showed me the light of the escape route. It came through the Word of God, and I am so grateful for His work in my life. I'll never be able to thank Him enough for His mercy and kindness He has extended toward me. He really does want our hearts to hear Him, and hear Him clearly. Therefore, I understand that excitement completely when from the depths of their hearts people begin to praise the Almighty.

> Being confident of this very thing, that he which hath begun a good work in you will perform it until the day of Jesus Christ.
>
> —PHILIPPIANS 1:6

My Bible has a center reference and lists "complete" as a substitute for the word *perform. He who has begun a good work in us will complete it.* Isn't that glorious? But listen to me. He doesn't just complete it on His own; He requires our participation. He completes it as we release our faith in the area that needs completion, as we continue to trust Him and stay pressed in to Him. We cannot expect God to start a work in us and then, while we live like an idiot, the work gets completed. We have to guard, not only what He's doing in our lives, but also what He's already accomplished in us. When the crises of life come our way, those times when we will either sink or swim depending on whether or not we believe God will complete the work He has started in us and that He will not forsake us in the midst of any situation. It is easy to say all the right things when life is smooth, but when we get under pressure, our real beliefs come forth, and that is what we will begin to speak out.

It is also true that our families get tuned in to our nature, habits, and reactions. They know how to "read" us, so to speak. Sometimes, they have to walk on eggshells because they are concerned we are going to unleash our mouth on them. One day we bless them and the next day we curse them. We act like we are serving God, being so holy doing all of these things at church, but in reality our family is afraid of us. Something is terribly wrong with that.

Listen, people are peculiar. They want us to love God, but do not really want us to love Him more than they do because they think it makes them look bad, or it makes them feel bad and often act as if they are not growing in the things of God. When we start applying the blood of Jesus to our lives morning and evening, we need to keep it between ourselves and God for a while. Let those deep changes of our heart bubble to the surface and affect our behavior for them to see. While they might be skeptical at first, before long they will see the glorious changes that God is working in our lives. Oh yes, we can change. If God can change me, He surely can change you.

> Ah LORD God! behold, thou hast made the heaven and the earth by thy great power and stretched out arm, and there is nothing too hard for thee...Behold, I am the LORD, the God of all flesh: is there any thing too hard for me?
>
> —JEREMIAH 32:17, 27

Is there anything too hard for our God? Absolutely not. I will tell you right now, it is too hard for you and it is too hard for me, but nothing is impossible for Him. He can touch us way down at the deepest levels, in the remote chasms, in the dark places of our hearts, and He knows exactly what needs to be done in every area of our lives. He is constantly working in us to perform what He has started in us. The greater One lives in us. If we can believe that, and I mean sincerely believe that, then it becomes a huge revelation in itself. Then, we can begin to see our entire nature change.

There is something that really bothers me within the church body. From a platform in the front of a church you can see a lot of things. You can see the people and their actions from a vantage point that is very enlightening as to their character. Some continually look at their watch—not conspicuously of course—during our services. They are the ones who are so anxious to get out of church, yet a lot of times, they are the ones who have the biggest problems. Does that make sense? I see people who do not care whether their nature is ever changed or not, people who are perfectly satisfied with their roughness and gruffness and their tepid dedication. Some are unconcerned if they offend everyone in their path or if they act like bullies. That upsets me so!

It is sickening to me when I hurt someone or when I offend some precious person. I certainly do not mean to do it, but there it is…the damage of my old nature raising its ugly head. When my life does not show forth the glory of the Lord, it hurts me. Appalled at my own actions, I am grieved because I've not been the witness that Jesus so needed me to be. I know you are the same; we both want to have God's heart and shine forth His goodness. We want to respond as He would, not as an unregenerate person. He did not belittle people, yell at them, or gossip about their actions to others. He just loved them. Surely, He confronted people, but that, too, was out of love.

This revelation is so exciting to me. I have things in me that I hate, and to think I can be completely free not only from the sin, but also its defilement and its power, is almost beyond my comprehension. Let's put on the priestly garment, come before God boldly as He has instructed us, and apply the blood, morning and evening, with the words of our mouth to our own heart and the hearts of others. It will wash away the stains and heal the wounds that we have so cleverly hidden from everyone except God. He's known about them all along, and He has wanted to set us free. Finally, we must allow Him to deliver us by working with Him, not against Him. It is all because of the shed blood of our beloved Lord Jesus Christ.

Let me just say this, being called a Christian doesn't make us a Christian. The name doesn't mean anything if we are not exemplifying the Lord and His nature. Wearing a cross doesn't make us a Christian. I have seen some shady characters with a big, gold cross around their necks who looked at me with scorn when I said to them, "Oh, you're a Christian?" Nope, they were just wearing the cross.

Let me share an incident that makes my point quite well. I was talking to a woman who worked at a local hospital. I happened to mention that one of my members worked in her department. I began to describe this woman's physical characteristics to her. I went on, "She's so nice. Active in church services, she's one of the sweetest ladies." This woman looked at me kind of stunned. "I know a woman with that name, who looks like the person you are describing, but I do not know the woman you are talking about. The woman that works in my department has a foul mouth and a sharp tongue. As a matter of fact, nobody wants to have anything to do with her. I think, perhaps, we are speaking of two different people." The sad thing was, we weren't. We were actually talking about the same person. She was one way in church, and another way at work.

We have to grab hold of these truths and really do this thing, my friends. The world needs what Jesus has provided, but we have to get it first. I know I have been redundant over many topics in this book. I have purposely stated the same things in as many different ways as I can think of. We must get this. This is an answer for the hurting and the wounded. Though forgiven, we have been as dirty and common as the world because of past sins. No wonder we have not been able to really impress anyone with our Christianity. But things can change, and they can change dramatically. There is hope for our hearts. Thank God. I want to plant in your soul a hope—an exceeding great hope—a hope that cannot easily be quenched. Grab hold, let it grow, and do not turn loose of it in the name of Jesus Christ, our Lord.

The devil will be the first one to tell us this thing does not and will not work. He whispers things like, "How many times have you already prayed? How many tears have you cried…and nothing has changed? What kind of a Christian are you anyway? You are still doing the same dumb sin." So we go down to the altar again at church and cry until we "feel" better. We thank God, walk out of the church talking to ourselves about how we are going to do better…how we are going to get a handle on things…how we are going to make this thing work. Do you understand? That is works— what we are going to do in our own power—not grace. Our flesh will always fail us. We cannot rely on it or our good intentions; it is not a matter of us trying harder. I've tried so hard it is just downright pitiful. I have tried endless times, but it did not get the job done. I was still a mess. See, it is not a matter of us—it is a matter of Him and what He has done for us. Without doubt, that is a different ball game. In Him we can win every time.

Without fail, we all want to be vessels of honor for God and uplift the name of Jesus with our lifestyle and conversation. True born-again Christians do not want to be hypocrites—individuals who say one thing and do another and do not walk what they preach. Many times I have heard people say, "I am not going to church. They are just a bunch of hypocrites down there." Occasionally, they are right. We say "Love, love, love," but treat everyone around us unkindly. We act spiritual, but have not opened our Bible in months. Help us, Jesus.

People act like hypocrites sometimes because they are not acting like true Christians. This is because they don't know who they are in Christ Jesus. They do not know or understand what He accomplished for them on the cross. Nor do they know their rights and privileges in Christ, or how to apply the blood of Jesus and let Him take care of their sin nature. Not knowing these things is against what our born-again spirit desires, I assure you.

The more I apply the blood to my heart, the more sickening it is to me when I find myself not walking in the things of God, so I continue to apply faithfully the blood. To be quite honest, the power of the blood of Jesus holds our greatest hope of ever being conformed to the image of the Lord Jesus. We have all wondered from time to time if God was on vacation, and did not really care if He stayed gone a while. Come on. We all get those thoughts. Depending on how deceitful our heart is, it may take several months of faithful application of the blood to see any results at all—but hang in there. Do not stop. We will begin to see a softening take place in our heart, a desire to know God in a much deeper way and serve Him. Perhaps sporadically at first, compassion will begin to manifest much to our own surprise. The blood of Jesus will soften our crusty heart so we can be tender toward Him and His desires for us and others.

Release your faith and begin speaking every day:

Thank You, Father, that my heart is getting soft. Thank You that my old, evil heart of unbelief is being transformed by the blood of the morning and evening Sacrifice. Thank You for changing my heart so that it is tender toward You. Glory to God! Please wash me, cleanse me, rearrange me, and change me. My heart longs and hungers for the things of God. I will see into Your kingdom; my eyes do see and my ears do hear. The voice of strangers I will not follow. Because of the change You are making in my heart, I have the mind of Christ, and I will obey Your voice quickly. Out of my mouth like a fountain come words of life to others that are hurting.

When we confess these types of things, we may not immediately begin to release our faith because sometimes we simply do not believe those confessions yet, but we will if we keep saying them. We need to speak what we desire according to Mark 11:23–24.

> Looking for that blessed hope, and the glorious appearing of the great God and our Saviour Jesus Christ; Who gave himself for us, that he might redeem us from all iniquity, and purify unto himself a peculiar people, zealous of good works.
>
> —TITUS 2:13–14

This Scripture passage declares emphatically that when I apply the blood and I realize that the iniquity issue (the sin nature) has been resolved and conquered that we will be zealous for the things of God. What does that mean? It means that we will want to serve God and will be hungry for the things of God. Our heart's cry will be, "I want to be in Your Word. I need to know the Your Word and Your heart, dear Jesus." These things bring life to us…they bring hope to us. How many have taken their own lives because they thought they had no hope of escaping their problems or sins? Too many did not hear this good news in time, I am sorry to say. I want to shout it from the housetops—*The blood is bigger and greater than any problem!* Even though at times it may seem impossible, there is no impossible situation when we get God involved. When we try to hide sins instead of facing and dealing with them head on, the pressure gets worse. Guilt and shame rise up in fury. We do not want to do that thing, but we haven't been able to conquer it. We become afraid that we will be judged because we cannot turn it loose. Yes, regrettably some will judge. The funny thing is, even though they have their own problems that they aren't dealing with, they will always have something to say about our failure.

The devil will use anything to destroy us, anything at all. But, our eternal destination is based on our belief in and receipt of God's salvation.

eleven

Standing in Confidence

Seeing then that we have a great high priest, that is passed into the heavens, Jesus the Son of God, let us hold fast our profession. For we have not an high priest which cannot be touched with the feeling of our infirmities; but was in all points tempted like as we are, yet without sin.

—HEBREWS 4:14–15

THANK GOD WE HAVE A High Priest that can help us. It is fabulous to know that we are not in this world as orphans, floundering without assistance. We have help in high places. Praise God forevermore. We have all been living far beneath our privileges, but Jesus is there to help us. He's there to lift us up and give us victory over every problem that we face. Glory to God!

> But Christ being come an high priest of good things
> to come, by a greater and more perfect tabernacle, not
> made with hands, that is to say, not of this building;
> Neither by the blood of goats and calves, but by his
> own blood he entered in once into the holy place,
> having obtained eternal redemption for us. For if the
> blood of bulls and of goats, and the ashes of an heifer
> sprinkling the unclean, sanctifieth to the purifying of
> the flesh: How much more shall the blood of Christ,
> who through the eternal Spirit offered himself without
> spot to God, purge your conscience from dead works to
> serve the living God?
>
> —HEBREWS 9:11–14

The people were looking for the Messiah. They were look-ing for somebody to come and set up God's kingdom. The word *Christ* means "Messiah, the anointed One." So here in verse 11, we have an acknowledgment that the Messiah has come. He came as a High Priest of good things to come. He did not come with bad things, but good things; and you and I need to find out what those good things are. At the top of the list is the blood He poured out, not only at Calvary, but on the heavenly mercy seat. That blood brings forth good things. Hallelujah.

In verse 14, the word *conscience* means "the thoughts and attitudes of the heart." Anybody have problems with them? We all do. So these scriptures are saying that the blood of Jesus can purge our thoughts and attitudes. It can totally cleanse our wicked heart (soulish area), our deceived *and deceiving* heart. The blood can purge our heart of dead works so that we can serve the living God. The blood can change the way we think if we apply it to our hearts. We can go free if we give Him something to work with and then let Him do it.

But this scripture also says to me that if our conscience is not purged, we cannot serve God. If our thoughts and attitudes have not been changed, we are restrained from fully serving Him. This is serious business, isn't it? We are not a little island unto ourselves or a little fly on the wall going through life. We are here with destiny in our blood—His blood flowing through our veins. We must think His thoughts, and thank God, He has given us a way to do that.

Jesus fulfilled the law for us. We are not under the letter of the law, but under the law of the Spirit of life in Christ Jesus. He has set us free and paid the ransom; we have been redeemed, justified, and made righteous by His blood.

> Cast not away therefore your confidence, which hath great recompence of reward. For ye have need of patience, that, after ye have done the will of God, ye might receive the promise. For yet a little while, and he that shall come will come, and will not tarry. Now the just shall live by faith: but if any man draw back, my soul shall have no pleasure in him. But we are not of them who draw back unto perdition; but of them that believe to the saving of the soul.
>
> —HEBREWS 10:35–39

This passage of Scripture is along the same lines. If our thoughts and attitudes are not purged by the blood, then we will cast away our confidence and we will not be able to stand. We will draw back unless our heart is cleansed. We have to believe in the saving of our soul, by faith, for the just live by faith. By faith, we believe what the blood will do for us, that it will cleanse our thought patterns so they will line up with the will of God and the ways of God, and enable us to stand strong without drawing back from Him. That is only done by faith in the Word of God.

> Whereupon neither the first testament was dedicated without blood. For when Moses had spoken every precept to all the people according to the law, he took the blood of calves and of goats, with water, and scarlet wool, and hyssop, and sprinkled both the book, and all the people, Saying, This is the blood of the testament which God hath enjoined unto you. Moreover he sprinkled with blood both the tabernacle, and all the vessels of the ministry.
>
> —HEBREWS 9:18–21

We are making comparison to what Jesus did and what Moses did because, remember, Jesus fulfilled the old covenant. So what Moses did in the natural, Jesus did in the spirit dimension. Can you understand that? It says that Moses sprinkled the book with blood. That would be the book of the law that they carried with them. It also says he sprinkled all of the people to cleanse them. "Vessels of ministry," is a key phrase, because in the spirit realm we are the vessels of ministry. Let's take a look at a scripture:

> Nevertheless the foundation of God standeth sure, having this seal, The Lord knoweth them that are his. And, Let every one that nameth the name of Christ depart from iniquity. [Do you see that? It says depart. It is the blood that will purge us from an evil conscience and allow us to walk free of the stains and power of sin. Hallelujah.] But in a great house there are not only vessels of gold and of silver, but also of wood and of earth; and some to honour, and some to dishonour. If a

man therefore purge himself from these, he shall be a vessel unto honour, sanctified, and meet for the master's use, and prepared unto every good work.

—2 TIMOTHY 2:19–21

We are the vessels of ministry, but it says we have to purge ourselves (v. 21) of sin and its residue with the blood to prepare us as a vessel of honor. If we do not apply the power of the blood and go through a cleansing of our heart, even though we are vessels of ministry, we will be one of dishonor. That choice is completely up to us. Almighty God has given us the key to move from dishonor to honor by purging ourselves with the blood of Jesus. Working with God, our hearts can be cleansed so we can serve Him honorably. That's glorious news. How exciting that our lives *can* change. There is hope for our heart. Praise God.

And almost all things are by the law purged with blood; and without shedding of blood is no remission. It was therefore necessary that the patterns of things in the heavens should be purified with these; but the heavenly things themselves with better sacrifices than these.

—HEBREWS 9:22–24

Many think we can act like the devil and God will open up His arms and say, "Come on in," when it cost the blood of His Son Jesus to purchase you and me. This is a serious matter.

And you, being dead in your sins and the uncircumcision of your flesh, hath he quickened together with him, having forgiven you all trespasses; Blotting out the handwriting of ordinances that was against us, which

was contrary to us, and took it out of the way, nailing
it to his cross.

—COLOSSIANS 2:13–14

But look what He did: He not only forgave our sin, made
us alive in Him, and raised us up to be with Him, He also
blotted out the handwriting of all the bad things that were
written against us. There is no record of any of it anymore in
heaven. His blood has wiped it clean. In other words, the Bible
tells me that He made it so, so that we could start out a life of
faith with a clean sheet. Our sins, though they are many, can
be washed away that we might be as white as snow. In God's
eyes, the residue of those former sins is not even there.

Apply the blood, dear ones, and walk free. Do not be
tormented another day, not one more hour. The precious
blood of Jesus has taken care of our sins and iniquities and
wiped away our yesterdays. God nailed it all to the cross, and
it died there that we could be made new. Hallelujah.

twelve

Free at Last

THE CROSS OF CALVARY WENT to the root of our sin problem and totally destroyed it. But is it working in all of our lives? I doubt it. Until we can grab hold of this truth and embrace it, our freedom from shame and guilt will still elude us. When we can begin to say, "No, no more. Sin, you no more have power over me. You are a snake whose head has been cut off by the power of almighty God. You're over there wriggling, trying to scare me, but I see you. You are acting like you're still alive and have control over me, but you are headless. Neither sin nor iniquity will control me anymore. Jesus is my Lord. As a priest before You, my Father, I apply the blood of Jesus to this sin and my heart. Dear Jesus, forgive me. Cleanse me from the stains and wounds that have haunted me. Create in me a clean heart, my Lord."

Do you know it takes courage to say those kinds of things and to make those types of declarations, especially if we continue to mess up? But that is what faith is—believing something we cannot see, and *seeing* in our spirit the things

115

that are not yet manifested. Can you see that? It does something to us when we keep doing the same dumb thing over and over again, whether it be temper, attitude, or sharpness of tongue, and it is terribly harmful. We have to break out of the rut, which takes courage, and faith in God and His glorious Word.

Faith is built on what we know. We use the term *blind faith*, but there is no such thing. Faith sees the end result based entirely on God's Word—the Holy Bible. God is not a man that He should lie (see. Num. 23:19), so trust Him. Let's build our faith on that Word by hearing it over and over again, and talk to ourselves saying, "My God took care of this sin. He also took care of the root of it. No, I am not going to spend the rest of my life acting like this. I am not going around this mountain forty times." Once that word—a *rhema* word—becomes a living part of us, our trips around the mountain will cease. Revelation can come quickly or it can be long and tedious depending on our decisions and how much time and attention we give the Word of God.

We know that by His stripes we are the healed, not the sick. Glory to God! Before getting that revelation, though, we all go around the mountain many times. That mountain of sickness is so well traveled that there is a rut there, a beaten path that holds us from breaking free. We have a lot of company going around that mountain, including family and friends. Think of how much time is spent conversing with each other about "our" sicknesses, and tending our sicknesses. No, Scripture says He bore "our" sicknesses. (See Matt. 8:17; Isa. 53:3–5; 1 Pet. 2:24.) Whatever sickness or disease is on us cannot be ours, because He bore our sicknesses.

We are so good at going around the mountain, we can go around even blindfolded, on one leg, even. Do you know a lot of people refuse to hear the great truth about healing? They do not want to get out of the rut, even when they can go free from sickness and disease. It is just too hard for them. Perhaps they get ridiculed by their family members, and they back off. Remember, many times when we decide to believe God, the religious people will not be happy.

We have not forgotten about Peter and the boat, have we? The Lord said, "Come." He did not say, "Peter, come" (Matt. 14:29). But Peter decided to step out and go to Him. All of the rest of the disciples probably said, "Peter, don't act foolish, get back in the boat. You're going to get in trouble out on the water. People can't walk on the water!" They all could have gotten out of the boat and experienced the miraculous, but only Peter made the move. Remember, Peter really did not walk on the water, he walked on the Word of God—"come." If we think everybody is going to be happy because we decide to go free by trusting God, we are mistaken. Surely you do not think the others in the boat said, "Oh, bless God, Peter, we are with you. Get in the water. We are with you, brother. You can do it. Go for it." Are you kidding? If they were saying that, they would have gotten out of the boat with him. No, Peter was on his own, and so are we sometimes when it is just God's marvelous Word and us. And in truth, that is all we really need—just a Word from God.

You know, Scripture states that the road leading to destruction is broad and there are many who are traveling it, but narrow is the one leading to everlasting life and few are they that find that path. (See Matt. 7:13–14.) Isn't that the same principle as the one I have been teaching? Hell is a real option, but we do not have to go there. Sickness is real, but we do not have to accept it. We often miss the mark and sin, but sin doesn't have to control us. The wonderful news is that we can walk away from all of that mess and live a glorious life, always submissive to God and believing His Word with all of our hearts.

Then why are people going to hell when Jesus doesn't want them to go there? Because they do not know or believe the provision that Jesus has shed His blood to redeem them from it. Why aren't we walking in victory from sin when the price has been paid to redeem us from it? Why do we let sin and shame rule and reign over us when Jesus is supposedly our King? Why do we bow our knee to things that we have already been redeemed from? We have all done it, at least in days past. We either do not know, or we do not believe what we do know enough to act on it. It is that simple.

I do not understand how He accomplished such an extraordinary freedom for us. It is miraculous; I do not even have the words to express how marvelous this is. But one thing I do know—*greater is He that's in us than he that is in the world* (see 1 John 4:4). And our God is not a man that He should lie. What God did, He did completely—and He did it for you and me because He loves us.

Things somehow change down in the deep places of our hearts when we get revelation that sin has lost its power over us. How long the sin and its wounds and defilements linger depends upon how long we allow it to do so. If we just put up with it, then we will keep it. At times, it is like we think we will have to twist God's arm to do something for us. We are so wrong. Our God is so loving, so kind, and so wonderful. He really does want us to be free, and we can walk in that freedom. We can stand firm and continue against all circumstances to proclaim our freedom—even though we are not acting free—and know the blood is working on our behalf. There is not a stronger power on this earth than the precious blood of our Savior, the Lord Jesus Christ. He is the *only* Savior. With all that He has done, how could we not love Him? How could we not be forever grateful for His mercy and grace?

Despite all of the provisions He has offered, there are some things that you and I need to do in order to enjoy the full wealth and benefits of the blood.

1. We have to have knowledge of its power and what the blood has done for us. We must understand it if we are to walk in the victory of it. There is far more removed from us than just the sin itself. God has done a tremendous work in our lives. He has restored us, healed us, annihilated our sin stains, and removed us from commonness. We are not common people, nor were we ever meant to be. Truly, if we do not know or believe that the stain has been removed, we are going to live as if the stain is still hanging over our head.

    Our unrenewed mind will be sure to keep us informed of its presence. Without knowledge, it is impossible to have faith, because faith comes by hearing. No hearing, no knowledge, and no faith will lead to—no action. We must earnestly grab hold of the words of hope and consciously lock onto them because we have an enemy that would steal them from us and keep us in bondage. If we have not made that determination, even though we have heard the teaching, we will continue to talk junk and continue to wallow in the same cesspool we have been in for years and years. It is a sad thing. We believe it is there and we "know" it is there. But it is really only in our head, because we have not allowed it to drop into our hearts or our spirits. Another option is to walk away from this book with our heads held high and declare to the heavens and anybody else who wants to listen, "I believe God. I believe Jesus died to set me forever free. I believe in the blood of the Lamb, and I apply it to my heart as the morning and evening Sacrifice. To His honor and glory, I will walk free."

2.   We must have a strong desire to fellowship with God, and to make the necessary changes to be well pleasing to Him. He has done so much for us. He deserves our allegiance and obedience, don't you think? He needs us to be vessels of honor; He has much to do in this final outpouring, and we are the ones who will ride in that destiny. Is it too much to ask of us? That surely is only our reasonable service.

3.   Cleansing cannot take place when there is not a complete separation from everything that is unclean. We cannot hold "clean" in one hand and "dirty" in the other hand. We must separate and consecrate ourselves to Him. Some of us have trouble because we have one foot in the world and the other foot over here in the church. That will not work, my friend. We will not walk in full victory unless we make a decision to turn loose of that old stuff.

The Bible says before God could bring the children of Israel into the Promised Land, He had to bring them out of Egypt. They could not enter the Promised Land while remaining in Egyptian bondage. Seems logical, doesn't it? But, look around. There are some who want everything God has to offer while trying to live in two places—church and sin. It is the same thing—that just will not work. We are not to touch the unclean thing; everything about us needs to go through the cleansing fire. It seems that the closer we get to Him, the holier we should feel. We actually feel dirtier because the light shines brighter and the fire gets hotter. We can see ourselves as we really are apart from Him, but there is no need to worry. He is the all-consuming fire. (See Zech. 13:9.)

4. We must exercise faith in the power of the blood because faith releases the power to work on our behalf and the behalf of others for whom we stand in the gap. Just because we have fifteen notebooks full of valuable notes means nothing if we do not allow the truth contained in those notes to penetrate and deal with our hearts. It does not matter how much we have danced and shouted because of this revelation, or how much our eyes have twinkled in excitement. If we do not apply the blood of Jesus by faith, it does not work. Do not ever say the Word did not work. All you are telling me is that you did not put it to work properly, or you did not give it enough time to work. *The Word always works when we put it to work in faith.*

Have mercy upon me, O God, according to thy lovingkindness: according unto the multitude of thy tender mercies blot out my transgressions. Wash me thoroughly from mine iniquity, and cleanse me from my sin. [David in essence said, "Get this thing out of me." God did it, because David never did that act again.] For I acknowledge my transgressions: and my sin is ever before me. Against thee, thee only, have I sinned, and done this evil in thy sight: that thou mightest be justified when thou speakest, and be clear when thou judgest. Behold, I was shapen in iniquity; and in sin did my mother conceive me. Behold, thou desirest truth in the inward parts: and in the hidden part thou shalt make me to know wisdom. Purge me with hyssop, and I shall be clean: wash me, and I shall be whiter than snow. Make me to hear joy and gladness; that the bones which thou hast broken may rejoice. Hide thy face from my sins, and blot out all mine iniquities. Create in me a clean heart, O God; and renew a right spirit within me. Cast me not away from thy presence; and take not thy holy spirit from me. Restore unto me the joy of thy salvation; and uphold me with thy free spirit. Then [When? When I am cleansed and the joy is there, and I am being upheld.] will I teach transgressors thy ways; and sinners shall be converted unto thee. [Do you know why? We need multitudes to teach people the ways of God and what He has done in our lives.] Deliver me from bloodguiltiness, O God, thou God of my salvation: and my tongue shall sing aloud of thy righteousness. O Lord, open thou my lips; and my mouth shall shew forth thy praise. For thou desirest not sacrifice; else would I give it: thou delightest not in burnt offering. The sacrifices of God are a broken spirit: a broken and a contrite heart, O God, thou wilt not despise.

—Psalm 51:1–17

Father God, we come to You in the name of Jesus, our Lord. O God, we thank You for the cross of Calvary and the precious blood that was shed upon that cross just for us. That blood reaches to the highest heights and flows to the lowest depths of our being. That blood enables You to forgive us, and we are grateful. It cleanses and sets us free from the bondage and struggles of sin and the residue that sin leaves behind. You have made us a holy people—a chosen generation. By Your grace and mercy, You have made us kings and priests to stand before You. Help us Lord Jesus to achieve the high calling You have commissioned us to fulfill. As priests, Father, we apply the blood of Jesus to our hearts. Soften them, mold them, change them, and cleanse them in us. May we truly walk free from the hauntings of our past so that we may truly exemplify Your goodness to the world. By Your precious Word, we can be what You say we can be, and do what You say we can do. Thank You for setting us free, dear Lord. We lift up Your church, those called by Your name. May divine expectation rise up within us. There truly is hope for our hearts. We really can go free from our past. Thank You. In Jesus' name, Amen.

This is a very personal thing, my friend. I cannot do it for you, and you cannot do it for me. We can preach to each other and offer it to each other with open hands, but in the end, it is a personal thing. I pray that each of us will gain the courage, the steadfastness, and the faith to take hold of these fabulous truths. Open your heart to Him. Allow the blood to flow into the dark places and open wounds that you have protected by locks and bars. Walk free at last because, glory to God, there is hope for the heart!

> And I will cleanse them from all their iniquity, whereby they have sinned against me; and I will pardon all their iniquities, whereby they have sinned, and whereby they have transgressed against me. And it shall be to me a name of joy, a praise and an honour before all the nations of the earth, which shall hear all the good that I do unto them: and they shall fear and tremble for all the goodness and for all the prosperity that I procure unto it.
>
> —JEREMIAH 33:8–9

Amen.